Literacy from Day One

Pat Barrett Dragan

HEINEMANN
Portsmouth, NH

Heinemann
A division of Reed Elsevier Inc.
361 Hanover Street
Portsmouth, NH 03801–3912
www.heinemann.com

Offices and agents throughout the world

Library of Congress Cataloging-in-Publication Data
Barrett Dragan, Patricia.
    Literacy from day one / by Pat Barrett Dragan.
        p. cm.
    Includes bibliographical references and index.
    ISBN 0-325-00343-2 (alk. paper)
    1. Reading—Parent participation. 2. Reading (Elementary). 3. Children—Books and reading. I. Title.

LB1573 .B36 2001
372.6—dc21   2001024855

Editor: Lois Bridges
Production editor: Sonja S. Chapman
Cover design: Joni Doherty
Cover photo: Pat Barrett Dragan
Manufacturing: Steve Bernier

Printed in the United States of America on acid-free paper

05 04 03 02 01 VP 1 2 3 4 5

To my husband George and my family, especially Mom, Sherry, Jim, Debi, and Marsha. And, of course, to Kay Goines.

Contents

Acknowledgments

I wish to thank Kay Goines, educator, children's literature specialist, and dear friend, for inspiration throughout my teaching career. I thank Gloria Norton, professor of education, San Francisco State University, for facilitating the connection with Heinemann. Many thanks to my editor, Lois Bridges, for such perceptive and sensitive help and encouragement. Thank you to Sonja Chapman, my production editor, and to Joni Doherty for such a beautiful cover. Thanks to Phil Erskine, who kept my computer running when it seemed impossible. A special thank-you to my mother, who listened, and Marsha Oviatt, who listened and advised. And heartfelt thanks to my husband George, who is as excited about this book as I am.

Introduction

Read aloud to children so they have a language they can trust to help them learn to read and write.

—Kay Goines

Do you remember a magical moment from childhood when you were looking at a cereal box or a sign or a book and all of a sudden you just *knew* what those marks, those words were saying? As primary teachers we help these discoveries happen. We help children learn to read, and sometimes we get to experience once again those magical moments, those epiphanies, as they happen to children in our classrooms.

How do we assist children in their learning, so that these discoveries happen? How can we facilitate this magical process of becoming literate? Studies universally show that readers are created when we read, read, and read to children.

I start reading to my first graders right away, the first morning, the first few minutes we are together. The stories bind us as a group and give us common memories. They help us to find our way to work together, to become a school family as we celebrate books and head toward literacy.

Of course, whatever age we teach, children come to us with varied abilities. Some can actually read and comprehend, while others are not yet sure what those alphabet letters are, or that letters can have sounds; that they form words. Many children come to us in an anxious state because they know they are supposed to learn to read here, and they don't want to miss it when it happens. Some even fear that it won't happen. I really don't want children to know if they can't read. I think it is important that they think they can.

When I lived in Massachusetts for a brief time, my friends took me ice-skating. They held me up, one on each side of me, and I actually skated, which had seemed to me to be an impossible undertaking. After a while I realized that they weren't there any more, and that I was still skating—all by myself! I want children in my classroom to come to literacy in that same way. I want them to think they are reading, be ready for it to happen, and then when reading sneaks up on them, know they can do it!

I tell my first graders that it took hundreds, even thousands, of years for people to be able to make sense of little marks written down on stone or paper. It also took an incredible amount of time for people to learn to make marks that meant something to someone else. I tell the children they will be able to understand and make marks with meaning—read and write—*this year*—starting right away, in fact.

Reading and writing are powerful inventions. They changed the world forever, just as the first graders who master these skills will be changed forever. One of my goals as a first-grade teacher is to help children believe, on the first day of school, that they *can* "read," *can* make sense of some little marks on paper. I want children to feel, as they leave the classroom that first day, that the burden has been lifted: They no longer must worry about "When will I learn to read?"—they have started to do it—the literacy process has begun.

This book is about some powerful ways to help children come to literacy. The seed idea was planted in 1977 when I took my first university extension course with Kay Goines, a Carmel, California, educator and children's literature specialist. I learned about her Overnight Book Program of sending a book home nightly with each of her kindergarten children so they could have the books read to them at home. I was excited about this idea, but full of trepidation. I wanted so much to fashion my own version of a book take-home program, but I had many questions:

- How could I manage such a program on a limited income?
- Where would I get enough quality literature and picture books to run a program?
- How could I manage the program in such a way that my precious books were returned to me in one piece, and were not lost forever?
- How could I set up a program without using up a giant part of each school day in keeping track of which child had which book?

I felt very strongly as a first-grade teacher wishing to convey to each child the gift of reading that the best and most powerful thing I could do would be to share my own books to be read aloud nightly. It was like saying, "This is the most precious thing I can do for you—teach you to read. And here are my very own books to help you with this task, so that your parents can read aloud to you each night, and soon you will be able to read the books too."

I struggled with organizational ideas. I took more courses from Kay Goines, and became more confident of my ability to select quality children's literature. I haunted garage sales, library sales, and bookstores. Finally, I decided to just jump in and begin the program and work out the details along the way.

This project metamorphosed into my version of Kay Goines' Overnight Book Program. It has been the cornerstone of my teaching, for as time went on, an amazing thing happened. Everything I taught began to connect with this program: literature and poetry charts, learning games, literacy center activities, illustrated photo poetry books, and literary calendars. I could even combine some social studies, science, and math activities. The literature became the hub of the day, because all of the curriculum could be integrated with it. I extended the program further into curriculum areas than I would have thought possible.

The Overnight Book Program truly has become the heart and soul of my classroom. It encompasses care and value of books, responsibility, and working together to learn, as well as such traditional curricular areas as phonemic awareness, phonics, language development, word recognition, vocabulary development, comprehension, sense of story, retelling, and so on. I feel I can teach just about anything by relating it back to the books and stories we love and enjoy as a group.

This book details how to create and maintain a classroom Overnight Book Program—not just how to start the program and continue it through the year, but also how to take advantage of the many learning opportunities that occur naturally as part of the program. It also describes the joys that such a program can bring to the classroom environment, as well as how it contributes to children's academic growth.

The program can be run and managed simply—but it takes trial and error to get to that point. I have tried a multitude of different management techniques and have worked the bugs out of the one I use. Teachers will want to find the organizational style that best suits them. This book describes a variety of management techniques.

I have spent many school years fine-tuning my literacy ideas, and I wish to share my journey with other teachers.

1

Getting Started on the First Day of School

The more we read together, together, together
The more we read together
The happier we'll be!
　　　　　—Adapted from Traditional Song

The first-grade school year has just ended, and I am leaving a roomful of readers—children who can't wait to see what's in the new books I bring in, who read independently, and who value books and reading. This class can't pass the Caldecott poster in the school library without stopping to excitedly name all the books they know and love. Each morning they anticipate the books they will take home "for overnight." They have written letters to next year's first graders. One of the things almost all of them wrote: "You will learn to read." As I look back over the year I am thrilled to see how far these children have come.

Coming Together as a School Family: Starting the Year

When the school year began in late August there were only five or six children who knew the alphabet or any letter sounds. Only four children were native English speakers. At least four different languages were spoken in the homes of children in the class. There were several transfers from other schools, and many behavior problems. We began working together as a literature group immediately, a few minutes after the children entered the classroom. We gathered together on the rug, enjoyed a story, and talked about it. We said poetry together and played with it, chanted it, and mimed it. We learned each other's names and talked about how the names looked and what letters they contained. Even before recess we had built some memories together and were on our way to becoming a school family.

Since attention spans are short, the beginning days of school are a constant back-and-forth between activities—stories, talking, poetry, movement, drawing, writing, singing. I have many things planned and many picture books and poems picked out so that I can easily move to a different activity when I see that the children need to switch gears.

Learning Names

I keep a pocket chart in front of the classroom by my chair. Near it I keep an alphabet strip, double sets of lowercase alphabet letters, a set of capital letters, and double sets of manila tagboard strips with the children's names on them. Right away we can use these cards for reading the children's names, matching name or alphabet cards, and spelling names with the alphabet letters. Names are of great interest to first graders. These name strips may be used to choose students for lining up, for passing out materials, for grouping, and for jobs and games. There is a lot of anticipation among students looking to see if their names have been selected for jobs or activities. A third set of names is available for the top of each child's desk. Later in the year we will have "name days" and enjoy writing each other's names.

Grouping Reading Materials

Books are all over the classroom, organized in tubs and baskets, on bookshelves, and in assorted book display racks with covers facing out. There are a variety of magazines. Many stuffed animals stand with their favorite picture books: A toy bat puppet hangs over Janell Cannon's book *Stellaluna*; stuffed "wild things" hover around Maurice Sendak's classic *Where the Wild Things Are*. A stuffed dog and a basket of other items hold John Burningham's *The Shopping Basket*. Two bears, one large, one small, sit with *Can't You Sleep, Little Bear?* by Martin Waddell, and Madeline and Curious George sit with their respective picture books. A tubful of other book characters and animals sits nearby.

These groupings change, and are frequently rearranged by the children and by me, depending upon what we are reading; what we are enjoying as a roomful of readers. The books and stuffed characters are not decorations. Sometimes these stuffed animals and figures are used to act out the stories. They are real to us; they become real as children hear and read and retell the stories. They play a large part in the imaginative life of the classroom. The children *want* to learn to read, to be involved with books. These characters and books are visual metaphors of our work with literacy.

Making Wishes for the School Year

One of our first-day activities is to talk about wishes, hopes, and goals for the school year. First graders have some very specific ideas about school. Many assume

Figure 1–1. Teacher and children enjoy a book together

they are going to learn to read on the first day, and they want to be sure it happens so they can go home and let everyone know.

As the children talk about their expectations I write down their thoughts on a large chart. I point out a few things as I write, such as some capital letters, sounds, and letter names, then we "read" their words together. We talk about making pictures in our heads to visualize what these words mean. Sometime during the day we illustrate this chart. Each child makes a crayon or marking-pen picture about a hope or wish for the year. These are cut out and glued onto the chart. We refer to this chart and these illustrations often throughout the beginning of the school year.

Usually there are more illustrations than there is space on the chart paper. It is very effective to place this chart in the center of a bulletin board and pin or tack the remainder of the children's drawings around it. In this way all the children are represented, and almost immediately there is something up on the wall that matters to all of us.

Several times during the school year we will revisit the idea of learning to read, and the children will have time to articulate how *they* feel about reading and about learning to read.

Sharing Special Books

Whenever I read to children I want to celebrate reading—to enchant, enthrall—to make reading and story an irresistible, essential part of their lives. I always choose the books I read aloud carefully, but I spend even more time choosing books for the first day and the first week of school. I try to pick literature that subtly deals with beginning-of-school-year concerns, such as *Wemberley Worried* by Keven Henkes; *Willy Bear* by Mildred Kantrowitz; *Emily's First 100 Days of School* and *Timothy Goes to School* by Rosemary Wells; *Leo the Late Bloomer* by Robert Kraus; *When Will I Read?* by Myriam Cohen; and *King of the Playground* by Phyllis Naylor.

When I read aloud to children I introduce the title and the author, and explain (with my mentor, Kay Goines', words ringing in my ears) that "the author couldn't come today." Almost immediately the children are annoyed that "the author *didn't* come today." However, they do make the connection that books are written by people, people who also have lives and do other things besides write.

"Reading" Pictures

Before I read a book to the children we often take a "picture walk." We look through the book together, discussing what may be going on, commenting on pictures, characters, and setting, and making predictions. This technique is important to new readers because it gives them strategies to use to help them read. It is also important for children from homes where no one can read, or where no one can read English. It is an enjoyable activity and gives children time to give their own input and interpretations, and to talk about similar experiences.

I tell my first graders that children can "read" pictures better than most grown-ups can. I truly believe that many adults have forgotten how to use this skill. I remember having to relearn it when I first became a teacher.

When children are involved in a picture walk, they create possible text through their discussion of the pictures. They try to find as many clues as they can in the pictures, using the sequence and the structure of the book to help them interpret what is going on in the story. They are really *pretelling* the story. The pictures help them make sense of the story, help them learn the content, and ultimately help them learn language and learn to read. This focus on illustration teaches children about different art media, story sequence, illustrators' styles, and fine art. It also validates a skill they have and frequently use—creating a story scene with pencils, crayons, and other art media.

Learning About Authors

When reading to my first graders, as often as possible I tell them about the author and share a photograph. Frequently the back of a book jacket has a photograph of the author and biographical data. I share information about the illustrator as well. Children are always very excited when we find this kind of information on the book flap or the back of the cover. Children's book club magazines typically feature author and illustrator interviews.

I make a point of sharing author and illustrator information with children because soon *they* will be authors and illustrators themselves. *They* will sit in the author/illustrator's chair in front of the classroom, or with a small group of children, and read their own stories and show their own art to a group of readers. I want children to make this "books are by people" connection right away because this concept makes the idea of writing, drawing, and *being* an author or illustrator very accessible to them.

Using Engaging Literature and Songs

Nursery rhymes and poetry are some of the most important literature for children to experience. The rhyme and rhythm are infectious; the words and visual pictures they evoke live easily in the mind and heart. Using poetry and nursery rhymes gives children an active break from sitting and listening. These activities develop language and the rhythm of language in a meaningful way.

Music is another activity that extends and enhances the literature experience. Many songs are good literature extensions, as well as being important activities in their own right. Some picture books are songs, such as *Wheels on the Bus: The Traditional Song*, pop-up edition, adapted and illustrated by Paul O. Zelinsky, and *Five Little Ducks* by Raffi. Music-based picture books have a powerful impact on children and can play a large part in helping children learn to read. If children know the song and can track words by pointing to the correct ones as they say them, they have a wonderful way to practice reading all by themselves.

Using Reading as a Life-Shaper

When children commit to mind and heart the words to poetry, nursery rhymes, and songs, they are internalizing language. This skill will help them to read, to write, to articulate, and to *live*. I often tell children about the words I always recited when I was little, when I was frightened: a few lines from *Sir Archibald* by Wolo. In the picture book the main character, a little monkey named Sir Archibald, is very scared as he walks through a thick forest full of trees. He refuses to be intimidated. He shouts, "Don't hear you. Don't see you. You're nothing to me! And how in the world can a nothing scare me!" This logic made a lot of sense to me when I was small. I felt that if these words were good enough for Sir Archibald, they were good enough for me. I said them to myself when I needed them, protecting myself for years with words from a story I loved.

Repeating the excerpt from this picture book helped me through scary situations and strengthened my resolve when I was facing a difficult task. The words from *Sir Archibald* were a safety net for me—a way of nudging myself onward when frightened, of making sure I did my personal, honorable best. The book connected with my own being at a very deep level. It gave me a creative way to think about problems and a way to face them.

I shared this memory about *Sir Archibald* with educators in a children's literature class I was teaching. The next day several members of the group approached me individually and related that my story had been very meaningful. People told me personal experiences that they helped solve through a strong connection to a special book, book excerpt, or poem. Literature has that power for all of us. It helps us to know who we are, helps us to shape our lives, both as children and as adults.

Internalizing Poetry and Book Excerpts

The book excerpts I emphasize in the classroom are for me the words that are the heart of the book. Often the children and I look through books we love together, to decide which parts are the ones to commit to memory. We recite, repeat, and chant book excerpts in the same way we do with poetry, in spare moments, in "apt" moments, walking to the lunchroom or waiting for the bell to ring, loving the sound and rhythm as well as the meaning of the words.

Poetry and book excerpts are such an integral part of the daily life of our classroom that a casual happening will evoke a poem or an excerpt from a book. For example, I had read *Farmer Duck* by Martin Waddell (illustrated by Helen Oxenbury) to my class on several occasions. I had seen the children spontaneously act out the book during free-choice situations, and we had done it as a classroom group as well. An overworked duck is the main character in the book. This poor duck is doing all the chores on the farm while the lazy farmer lies in bed eating chocolates. At intervals the farmer will shout, "How goes the work?" and the duck shouts, with varying degrees of annoyance as the story progresses, "QUACK!"

I finished reading *Farmer Duck* and went over to sharpen pencils while the children were busy with other tasks. A child looked over at me and asked loudly, "How goes the work?" Several other children echoed the question.

"QUACK!" I replied, and we all broke up laughing. I felt that this was a very sophisticated literature response from six- and seven-year-olds. It was also an "in joke" for all of my first graders because of their deep connection to and common experience with a piece of literature they love.

One day, after we reread and enjoyed *Millions of Cats* by Wanda Gag together, the children asked to make a mural showing "all these cats." As a group, we decided to make the cats of torn paper and glue them to a mural with some of the words from the book.

As the children were tearing and creating their animals I could hear Sara singing, chanting, repeating over and over as she worked, "Hundreds of cats, thousands of cats, millions and billions and trillions of cats." Other children heard her and joined in. This is the book excerpt that we eventually chose to print on the mural with the multitude of torn paper cats.

"Reading" a Nursery Rhyme

Since children's expectations are that they will *read* on the first day of school, it is important to honor this need and provide for it. I like to use *Humpty Dumpty* for this activity because it is one of the nursery rhymes children are apt to know when they enter school. I begin reciting *Humpty Dumpty* to the children, and soon they are joining in. We talk about the rhyme, and the pictures they have in their heads when they hear and say the words. I show them the words on a poetry chart. I wait before I point out what these words are, and sure enough, some children begin puzzling out that this is *Humpty Dumpty*.

We "read" the chart together while I track the words by pointing to them as we say them. Then I read aloud Miko Imai's modern picture book about one of Humpty Dumpty's descendants, *Little Lumpty*. Little Lumpty has the same love of the wall as his famous ancestor, and climbs it against his mother's advice. However, Little Lumpty's mother is a divergent thinker. When her son is trapped on top of the wall, too scared to climb down, she calls for a blanket brigade and has him jump to safety. Children love both the book and the nursery rhyme, and the two pieces of literature work well together.

Using Nursery-Rhyme Booklets

After this read-aloud experience I show the class a folded paper booklet with the title *Humpty Dumpty* on the front cover and the nursery rhyme printed on the remaining three pages. I read it to them as they say the nursery rhyme with me. Then I give the children folded booklets and have them illustrate the poem with crayons, marking pens, or colored pencils.

After the children illustrate their *Humpty Dumpty* booklets we come back to the rug and "read" them together. I remind them how to track by moving a pointer finger under each word as they say the word. We praise each other and celebrate because we can all "read"!

The next step is to let the children know how to show off this new skill at home, or to whoever is picking them up after school. I pretend to be a first grader. I have one of the children pretend to be a parent saying, "Hi Honey. How was school? What did you do today?" (Children *love* to paraphrase and invent their own conversations.)

FIRST GRADER, PLAYED BY TEACHER, RESPONDING: "I learned how to read."
PARENT, PLAYED BY FIRST GRADER, ACTING ASTONISHED: "You did?"
FIRST GRADER, PLAYED BY TEACHER, RESPONDING: "Humpty Dumpty sat on a wall," etc. I "read" and track the *Humpty Dumpty* booklet, while the "parent" faints and falls to the rug.

We play this scene a few times with variations and different children, and enjoy it thoroughly. And, once in a while, I see this "I Can Read" scene reenacted between surprised parent and proud child in the classroom doorway at the end of the day.

Figure 1–2. Sabine reads *Humpty Dumpty* on the first day of school

Making Booklets I use four-page and eight-page booklets in my classroom for a variety of reading, writing, and other activities similar to the one described. The format for both booklets is simple: Both are made from a single piece of paper. To make the four-page booklet, fold a paper in half the long way. Fold it in half again, left to right. Now you have a small booklet with a cover and three additional pages. (See Appendix 3 for directions for the eight-page booklet.)

Creating a "Reading Is Fun" Poetry Chart

Like most teachers, I probably plan enough for the first day of school to take us through at least a week or two. One of my personal goals each year is to teach the children many poems and help them to have wonderful experiences with poetry. Many of the chants and poems I teach are meant to subtly imprint children with positive attitudes about books and stories and reading. I use this one on the first day of school:

> **Reading Is Fun**
> Reading is fun,
> Reading is fun,
> Reading is fun
> For everyone!
> The more we read,
> The better we read,
> So READ! READ! READ!

We recite these words together, enjoying an experience that I hope will shape lives and create readers.

Soon after the children learn this chant I show them a written version. As with the *Humpty Dumpty* chart, I do not introduce the words on the chart paper—I just hang the chart up and casually start another activity. Soon some of the children will realize that these are the words to the poem we just recited together. This is a big epiphany, a big "aha!" I point out to the children that in figuring this out they are *really* reading!

We celebrate this feat by illustrating the chart together. Each child does a drawing using such materials as crayons, marking pens, colored pencils, or a combination of these. The drawings are cut out and placed on the chart. Some are glued or taped on with tape rolls on the back of the drawing. Other illustrations are placed around the chart as it is hung on a bulletin board or wall. We refer to this chart often, and "read" it together, always tracking the words with a pointer.

Introducing the Overnight Book Program

I always let the children know about the Overnight Book Program right away—on the first day of school. In this program, each child chooses a book to take home "for overnight" for someone in the family to read aloud. Children are anxious to get this program started. This year one of my first graders calls it the "tonight book." "Overnight books" are kept on a specific display. They are books I have already read aloud to the students. As soon as I have read twenty to twenty-five books aloud to the class and have done some initial instruction with the children the program can begin. It will be one of the most important things we do all year.

2

Discovering the Ticket to Literacy—Books!

My Mom reads to me. And then after, when we get dinner, I go to sleep when my Mom reads to me.

—Oscar

The Reading Mother
You may have tangible wealth untold;
Caskets of jewels and coffers of gold.
Richer than I you can never be
I had a Mother who read to me.
    —Strickland Gillilan in *Best Loved Poems of the American People.*
                        New York: Doubleday, 1936

Experts worldwide agree that the way to help children become readers is to read aloud to them. Being read to is a special gift—the gift of time and attention, and of the delight in words and stories being passed on from one person to another. When we read aloud to children they assume that we value and approve of the story being read, so they value it as well. Books become associated with pleasant, enjoyable, even magical experiences. They can take us to other lands and pull us out of ourselves and into other worlds, other lives. They can stir our spirits, open us to new possibilities and new ways of thinking. And they can create strong bonds between reader and listener.

Children need to be read to from early infancy to long past the time when they can read for themselves. We talk to them and sing to them at birth and even before. Reading aloud is another wonderful way to communicate with our brand-new babies. The beautiful words of some picture books and poetry books can help infants learn how to talk and can help adults bond with our new infants. People of all ages, including many adults, read aloud to each other. It can be a favorite lifelong pastime.

Children need to be read to both at home and at school so that they can become readers themselves and learn to passionately value books and reading. Listening to stories they enjoy can help children develop their attention spans and listening skills. They internalize the rhythms and patterns of language, vocabulary, sense of story, and story elements. Reading imparts values. It builds knowledge and stimulates creativity. Children also learn about themselves and others through the book choices they make and the characters and books they love. The stories they hear and read as children can affect their thinking, interests, and attitudes far into the future—for the rest of their lives.

Introducing Overnight Books to Children

The Overnight Book Program is a way to provide books for children at home on a daily basis, books that have already been selected and read aloud in the classroom. Aside from the obvious goal of getting books into the hands of children and their parents, the program gives constant opportunities for meaningful literacy learning in the classroom. There are many skills and activities involved, from organization, responsibility, and writing to book title "scavenger hunts," word-matching games, recitation of favorite book excerpts, and reading independently.

I start from day one emphasizing wonder and delight in books and stories. Then I talk about the origin of books. I tell children that writing and paper had to be invented before there were books, and that early books were so valuable they were chained to library shelves. One thousand years ago most people had never even *seen* a book.

Selecting and Caring for Overnight Books

The first group of twenty to twenty-five overnight books is chosen with extra care: They are wonderful books and stories, but not the newest of my collection. Typically, a few books may have small repaired tears. I explain to the children that these books have been very loved and cared for by many, many readers and that we will treat them the same way. As each child chooses a preliminary book to practice book handling and making book choices, we find a few small tears. The children watch as I fix them. Quite soon, usually the first day or two, we discover a parent who will help out by fixing books. I send home wide transparent tape and we send severely damaged books to that parent's "book hospital" for repair.

When I talk about book care with children, I have already read the book. I point out the parts of the book: spine, cover, title page, frontispiece, end papers, and so forth. I show children directionality—reading from left to right, from the top of the page to the bottom. These are all concepts of print they need to know. I show them how to lift pages at the corner, and how to not "mash them like a potato" when turning them. We talk about not writing in books. I ask children to always let me know when they find a tear or something wrong with the book so that we can fix it before it gets worse. I show them how I erase pencil marks.

When children are not present I cover other marks in books with correction fluid. I also ask children to please let me know if something goes wrong at home and there are tears or marks in books (of course that wouldn't happen!) so that we can fix them together.

Limiting Book Choices

I limit the number of books available at the beginning of the school year so that children will have a focus of about twenty to twenty-five books—one per child and five or six extra. I can easily read that many aloud the first week, and we can begin the program the second week of school. With a limited number of books there will be a core of book experiences right away. We can talk about books and their authors and illustrators much more easily when there is a small, specific group of titles. The children have fewer titles to learn to "read" and "write." There are a restricted number of characters, settings, plots and adventures. As I read other books the second week of school and beyond, I may hold off putting them on the overnight bookshelves until a little later in the year.

If children seem to lose interest in the books available for take-home, I add other books to the shelves. I add only books that have already been read aloud to children. Depending upon the interest and focus of the group I may remove some books so that only twenty to twenty-five books remain, or I may increase the number. This is the way I handle changing the overnight book selections throughout the year.

Later in the school year some classes can handle, and desire, many book choices. Sometimes children ask that specific books be placed on the overnight-book shelves. Whenever possible I honor their requests.

Displaying Books

Books are much more appealing when their covers face outward. With a small number of books to choose from it is easy to place them so that their covers, rather than their spines, show. This makes choosing books much easier for children. Inexpensive cardboard book displays are available and work quite well for this purpose. Another possibility is plastic rain gutters fastened on the edges of bookshelves or window ledges, or on brackets on the wall. In this way many books can be on display at the same time. Books can also be leaned against the wall, face-out, under chalk trays, whiteboard pen trays, or bulletin boards.

Introducing the Program to Parents

The success of the Overnight Book Program depends upon parent involvement at home. There are many ways to introduce parents to the program. If you will be starting the program a little later in the school year, parent conferences or back-to-school nights are a good time to explain the program to parents. Letters sent home are another possibility. You may wish to casually talk about the program with a few parents at a time when they pick up their children after school. Another idea is to have a brief afternoon or evening parent meeting specifically about the Overnight Book Program. Even after meeting with parents I also send home a letter like this one:

Dear Parents,

As you know, one of the most important things we can do for our children is to read aloud to them. These read-aloud book experiences are wonderful parent-child sharing times, and will help your child to love books and to become a reader.

I would like to make my own books available to your family. I will be sending a book home each day with your child for someone in your family to read aloud. Your child has chosen the book with excitement and anticipation. I hope you will enjoy the book together!

Please help your child put the book and the booklist in the book bag and return it to school each morning.

Thank you, and happy reading!

_____(Your child's teacher)

Parents are anxious for their children to learn to read and do well in school. They are generally very willing to help the process if they know some ways to proceed. In addition to sending letters home, I meet with parents. I begin by explaining the importance of reading to children to create readers. I tell them their children will be picking a book each day for someone at home to read aloud: parent, sibling, aunt or uncle, cousin, or grandparent. We talk about the bonding experience of reading aloud to children.

I try to elicit information from the parents about things that they do when they read to their children. These tips can be helpful to everyone. Some parents are not comfortable reading aloud to their children and may benefit from seeing a teacher model reading aloud or from seeing a "read-aloud" video. These are available at public libraries. You may choose to show a classroom or school-made video showing a variety of teachers reading aloud to whole classes, small groups, and individual children.

I like to give parents a list of read-aloud techniques, including these:

- sit with the child or children in a comfortable place
- talk about the book and the illustrations
- encourage children to ask questions and make comments before and after the story is read
- relate the theme of the book to a special family experience when possible,

such as, "This looks like what happened to Grandma when she rode your bike!"
- talk about the characters in the story
- talk about the setting—the place where the story is happening
- predict story events: "What do you think will happen next?"
- sequence story events: "What happened first?" or "Before that?"
- point to words some of the time when reading
- enjoy the story together

I stress that not all of these things need to be accomplished each time a story is read. These are just a few guidelines to help create a meaningful read-aloud experience. All of this needs to be done casually, as part of a comfortable, intimate parent-child time together. Treating the whole experience as a test or teaching situation could spoil this special sharing time.

Retelling the Story

Talking with children after the story and giving them a chance to retell favorite parts and ask questions can be another important parent-child book-sharing activity. Children learn a lot about a story when they try to express it, to recreate it both in their own minds and aloud. Parents and children can learn a lot about each other through these shared experiences. This can lead to the telling of personal stories or family stories, strengthening bonds between parent and child.

Planning Times to Read Aloud

Many parents have unusual work hours and need to strategize to find times when they can read to their children. Some read at breakfast, or between cooking dinner and doing dishes. Others read after dinner or at bedtime. I suggest that parents set a regular time to read aloud to their children daily. Of course, more than once a day would be wonderful!

Taking a "Picture Walk"

Some parents cannot read, are not comfortable reading, or do not read the language used in the books that go home. A solution for this problem is the "picture walk."

The children know how to take a picture walk because we do it in the classroom before we read a book together. This technique could also be shown in a classroom or school-made video. In a picture walk at home, parent and child look through the book, talking about the cover and the illustrations. They talk about similar experiences, their ideas of what is going on, and what will happen in the story. The book's illustrations serve as "translators" for story events.

Wandering in a book's pages with this kind of scrutiny and enjoyment, parent and child bring meaning to the written words that they cannot read, and they have an intimate literary experience together. As time goes on, parents and children will both find that they can read some of the text. They will find that many of their predictions were correct. The child has already heard and discussed the story at least once at school. This knowledge adds to the understanding of the book at home.

Sharing a Read-Aloud Display

When I meet with parents I share an ongoing photographic read-aloud display of children from previous classes (and a few from my current class, if possible). This display is a bulletin-board grouping or chart of photographs showing children being read to at home. Some photos show a child being read to by a parent, grandparent, brother, sister, or other reader. Different photographs show a whole-family read-aloud scene. The important thing is the variety of experiences, the involvement, the sharing of the book.

The children and I build the year's chart together gradually as photographs are brought to school. We see all the children being read to in their favorite places in their homes. We see the books they love, and the people they love reading to them.

The photo display chart celebrates our reading experiences and shows parents possibilities for their own family read-aloud sessions. I want parents to see photos of a variety of read-aloud experiences to help them visualize themselves having similar experiences with their children in their own homes. When I meet with parents, the photo display helps clarify what is expected and what is possible when children bring their overnight books home.

Creating a Read-Aloud Display

To create our photo display chart each year, I send an inexpensive Polaroid camera home (in a padded backpack) with one child each night until all children have had a turn. The child is instructed in the use of the camera and about what is to be photographed—and that there is to be one photo only. Children like the feeling of taking the camera home and of being empowered to explain to someone that they are to take a photograph of someone reading aloud to the child. I also send a brief note to parents:

Dear Parents,

We are making a wonderful photo display chart at school full of photographs of the children in our class being read to at home. The children are taking turns

Figure 2–1. Photo display chart

bringing home the Polaroid camera for someone to photograph each of them being read to by a family member.

Today your child has brought home the camera. If possible, please arrange to have *one* photograph taken of someone reading to your child, or to all the children in your family. Please return the photo tomorrow, along with the camera, so that we can add this to our photo display chart.

I hope that you and your family will want to be part of our "Home and Family Reading" bulletin board. Thank you for helping us with our project. Please be sure to drop by our classroom and see the growing collection of photos of all the children being read to at home.

Sincerely,

_____(Your child's teacher)

This activity seems expensive, but the rewards are many. It requires an inexpensive Polaroid camera and enough film to take one photo of each child in your class. If you feel there is apt to be a problem with a child coming back with multiple photos, organize things so that this child will take the camera home when there is only one photograph left in the pack of film. If you feel the camera will never make it to the child's home in one piece, let alone back again, make arrangements with the parent, and possibly make this child the last one to be photographed. (Perhaps the parent could transport the camera, rather than the child.) Of course there is a risk of the camera getting broken. My Polaroid lasted over three years before it came back to school missing the viewfinder. I went right out and purchased another, because the photo display is an integral part of my program.

An alternative plan would be to purchase a disposable camera and have one picture a night taken. The film would be developed after all children had their photos taken.

Using Other Reading Strategies

I suggest to parents that, as well as reading to their children themselves, they encourage extended family—brothers, sisters, cousins, aunts, uncles, grandparents—to also read aloud and celebrate reading. This will give the child a chance to hear more reading models, and also provides more story-time experiences.

Tapes of stories are also helpful to send home with overnight books, as long as the tape coordinates exactly with the text of the book. I acquire some tapes along with paperback books from children's book clubs such as Scholastic, Trumpet, and Troll. Another way to get tapes is to make them.

Since time is always short in the life of a classroom teacher, I struggle to find a simple, fast way of making tape recordings for overnight books. Often when I am reading aloud to children I tape myself reading the book. Then I can use the tape at a listening center or send it home with the book. The tape will not be of perfect quality, but will be of some help to families with limited English. It also provides children with a way to hear their favorite stories again and again and again. I do not worry if I have tapes for only some of the books. The tapes are not meant to be a substitute for someone at home reading to the child.

Children often like to hear the same book read over and over. Parents need to know that this is important for the child. Children can learn a great deal from books and stories they listen to again and again. One of my first graders, Oscar, chose the book *Avocado Baby* by John Burningham almost every day of the school year. The book always enthralled him. He hugged it as he carried it from the classroom in his bookbag. On days when Oscar was ready for another kind of reading experience he picked a different story. As the school year ended he was still choosing *Avocado Baby* on a regular basis.

I tell parents that it is helpful to children if the reader holds the book in such a way that the child can see the words while listening to the story. The parent can also point to some words while reading. This is not always appropriate—for example, at bedtime when the child is drifting off to sleep.

When I talk to parents I show how stories can be reread, pausing at words and phrases or leaving them out, giving the child time to fill in those repetitious missing parts. Children enjoy filling in the missing pieces, especially with books that have predictable patterns. Other times, children simply want to hear the book again. One reading at a sitting may not be enough. There have been occasions in the classroom when I have just finished the last word of a story and one or more children spontaneously demands, "Read it again!" And I do.

Responding to Books

It is important to allow time for children to talk about the books read and ask questions. This helps children to connect stories and the characters in them with people and events in their own lives and in the world. It helps them make sense of what they have read or heard. However, there are times when children do not wish to talk about the story or the books they have listened to or read. It is crucial that this need be respected, and that we do not pry into children's private feelings. I like to let children take the lead here.

I find that my first graders have much to say spontaneously when I am introducing and reading a book. They comment about story events, characters, funny sounding words, rhymes, the illustrations, and so forth. They puzzle out things together, pooling the group's intelligence to make sense of the text and illustrations and make them relevant to their own lives.

I am always a little torn about how much of this to allow, because I do not want to interrupt the flow of the story. I do try to read a story uninterrupted the first time so children have a more holistic experience. However, I am realizing that giving time for children to talk freely and spontaneously and share *as they hear the story* keeps talk and thinking flowing. The kinds of discussions teachers would love to hear *after* a book is read do not always happen then—frequently they occur in the midst of the reading. It is then that the children delve for meaning together and struggle to express themselves, to make sense of the story. I want all the children to realize that there is meaning in the text between the covers of a book, and that they will enjoy the story much more if they think about it while it is being read to them. Then we have the fun of discussing the personal connections we made as we listened to the book.

A wonderful book to use for this concept of *meaning in text* is *Petunia*, by Roger Duvoisin. Petunia, the silly goose, finds a book in the barnyard. She becomes quite proud and carries it under her wing, because she has heard that books are equated with wisdom. She advises the animals in the barnyard about any and all matters and concerns. The book falls open due to an unfortunate accident caused by Petunia's "misreading" of the words on a mysterious package. It is only then that Petunia realizes that there are pages with words inside the book, pages with wisdom and meaning—and to find that meaning she must learn to read.

Balancing Talk and the Story

I try to keep aware of children's needs and to balance children's talk and the integrity of the story. This can often be done by reading the story a second or third time. Rereading a book takes them deeper and deeper into its language, mystery, and magic, and provides the delicious anticipation of hearing favorite words and phrases again and again. Enjoying stories over and over helps children make those important connections between books and their own lives, between books and the world, and between different pieces of literature.

Revisiting a Story

After a story is read it is helpful to give children the chance to revisit the story and to reread the book independently. Some children wish to try to read the book or parts of it aloud, or to alternate their reading with parents' reading. This is best after the initial reading of the book. Books need to be *readily available* to children after they are read aloud, both at home and at school.

Visiting Libraries and Bookstores

Trips to public libraries and bookstores are other ways parents can stimulate interest in reading. Many libraries and bookstores hold wonderful events for children: meet the author or illustrator programs, storytelling, read-aloud times, puppet shows, and so forth. Subscriptions to magazines and children's book clubs are also helpful ways parents can further the love of reading.

I can still feel the anticipation of being about to go out with my father on an occasional evening to choose a picture book or magazine. Part of the excitement of the experience was that it was unplanned, and it was also a special time I could be with my dad.

Exploring Environmental Print

Another very worthwhile activity at both home and school is to explore "environmental print" with children. These are the words found naturally all around us, on cereal boxes, stop signs, canned foods, billboards, and store fronts. Recognizing just one new word a day will add up fast. The learning is cumulative.

In the classroom I like to label things with the class: the wall, the computer, desks, doors, etc. It seems more powerful to do this *with* children rather than do it ahead of time *for* them. It is helpful to have extra sets of labels so children can match the word-label cards to the words around the room. This is an enjoyable literacy center activity. (See Chapter 7 for literacy center suggestions.)

Sending Books Home

There are many ways to send the books home overnight. Kay Goines always used large manila envelopes with lines she had drawn ahead of time with pencil or pen. Children use the lines to write the title of their selected book each day. When I began the program in 1977 I used these envelopes myself, but I found that my school could not supply enough of them, and they were too expensive for me. Teachers traditionally spend a great deal of their own money on their classrooms and their students. I choose to spend a minimal amount on ways to get books home, and more on the books themselves.

Another way I used the large manila envelopes was to laminate them, then slit them across the opening with a scissors. Laminated envelopes lasted quite a long time—most of the school year—but there was no place for children to write book titles. Writing book titles daily teaches children a great deal about reading and writing. It also provides an important record of the books each child has selected to take home. For a time I used a manila-folder booklist with lined papers stapled inside. These booklists were kept inside the laminated envelopes. My problem with these envelopes, laminated or not, was that many of my books are oversized and did not fit inside the envelopes. Very large envelopes fit the books but seemed unwieldy for the children. They are difficult to fit in desks and backpacks. And, of course, the very large envelopes are much more expensive to purchase.

I have met other teachers who run take-home book programs who have parents make denim book bags or backpacks. This seems like a good idea to me, but it does not quite fit my personal program.

I teach in a very foggy and drizzly climate. Laminated envelopes suited this situation. One year I used gallon-size plastic freezer bags for book bags. These worked, and lasted for quite a long time, but were not quite big enough for over-sized books. Then, through a stroke of luck, I was able to obtain plastic bags with closure strings from a shoe store. Last year in my classroom we used the shoe bags, and one bag per child lasted all year. Next year, now that I know how long these bags last, I will probably use them again. Another alternative I have thought of is to use extra-large plastic freezer bags that would accommodate oversized books. It is also possible to not include oversized books in the program.

Labeling the Book Bag

If plastic book bags are used, it is a good idea to tape a large label to the front of the bag. The label could show the child's name, school, and the words "Book Bag for Booklist and Overnight Book." This would help parents understand what is to go into the bag, and perhaps make it easier to oversee that the book bag is being used correctly, instead of as a repository for extra crayons, pieces of toys, or scraps of old homework.

A Sampling of Ways to Send Overnight Books Home

- large lined envelopes with book titles written on lines by children
- large laminated envelopes with booklists inside
- plastic freezer bags with booklists inside
- shoe bags or department store plastic bags
- parent or teacher-made or purchased cloth book bags
- large envelope donations from businesses
- children's own backpacks

Including Booklists

Booklists are a very important part of the Overnight Book Program. Each day children choose a book and write down the title on their booklist, using pencils or marking pens. This exercise of finding the title and writing it down is some-what complex when you consider the many fonts, graphics, and writing styles used on book covers. I like to show the children a variety of fonts on the computer. For booklists, I give each child a manila folder in which I've made pencil lines inside and out. When these lines are full of book titles I staple additional lined papers inside the folders. These booklists have worked well. One folder with additional stapled pages inside will last the school year. A booklist is an important record of a student's book choices over the nine- or ten-month period.

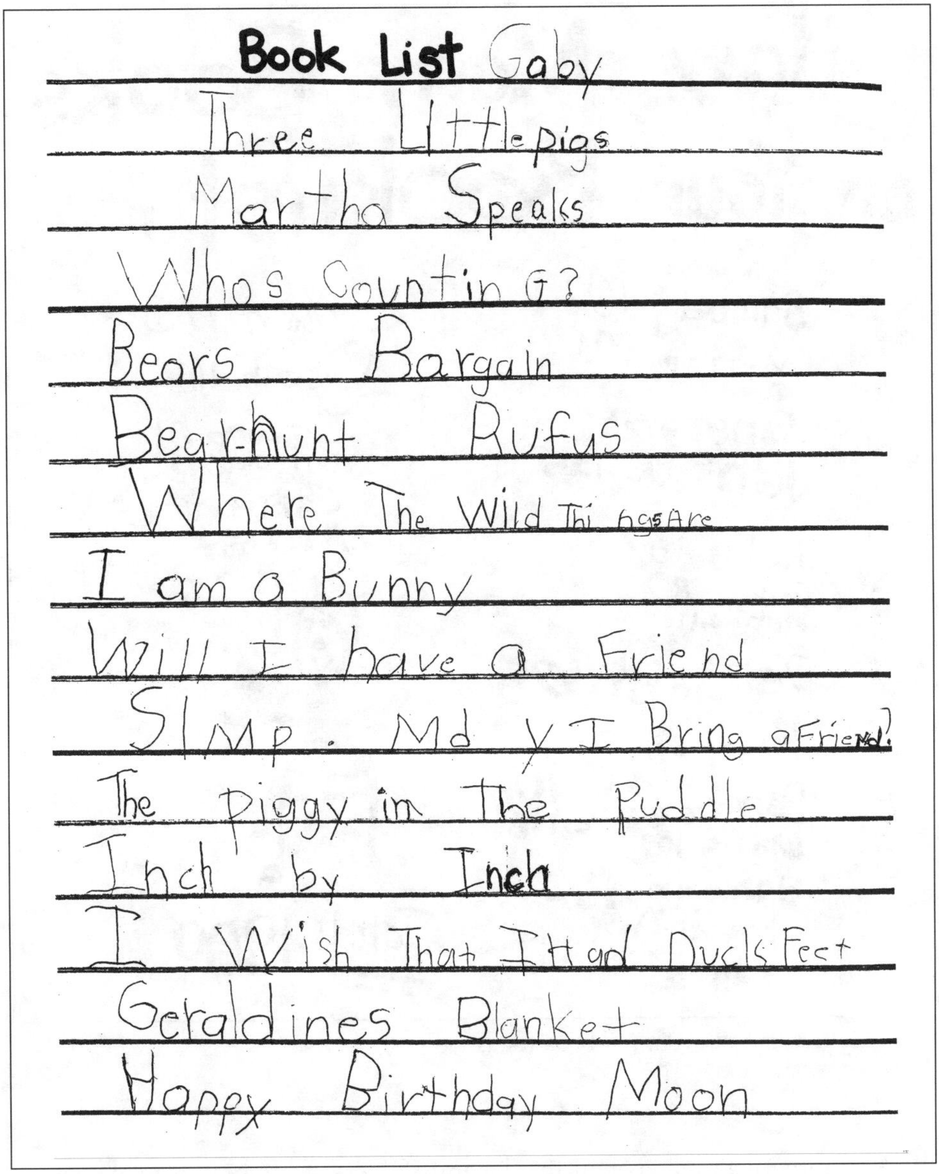

Book List Gaby

Three Little pigs

Martha Speaks

Whos Counting?

Bears Bargain

Bear hunt Rufus

Where The Wild Things Are

I am a Bunny

Will I have a Friend

SiMp. Md y I Bring aFriend!

The Piggy in The Puddle

Inch by Inch

I Wish That I Had Ducks Feet

Geraldines Blanket

Happy Birthday Moon

Figure 2–2. Sample booklist

How Many Books on Your Booklist?

Samuel 102
Myriam 101

JaneT 77
Jenna 125

Fabi 107
Sara 82
Brenda 118

Jeremiah 105

Francisco 106
Bernadette 116
Maria 109
Haneen 100
Keith 33
Edgar 102

Hugo 113
Oscar 107
Irving 81
Griselda 92
Christian 76
Alexis 57

Total: 1909

Figure 2–3. Chart of overnight book totals

An alternative to the pencil-lined manila folders, if you have a good copying machine at school, is to cut manila tagboard to eleven-by-seventeen inches, then run it through the copier to make lines on both sides. Fold it like a folder. Staple in additional pages as needed.

The child's booklist is a record of books read. At the end of the year we count the number of books on these lists and record how many were read aloud at home to the children. Last year we began the program later than usual because of packing and moving due to school renovation. Our end-of-the-year lists were still cause for celebration. The twenty children in the class, including two who moved early in the year, were read a total of 1,909 books!

This year's class takes great interest in our chart and these figures. Since our school renovation is over, the class began taking home overnight books the second week of school. After a little over three months of school the class total for overnight books read aloud to them at home is 1,140. If our overnight book program continues on schedule, this class of first graders will have listened to a total of 3,520 overnight books by the end of the school year in mid-June!

3

Managing an Overnight Book Program

I like to go to school because I can pick a book I like and I bring it home
and my Mom reads it to me and I bring it back and then I get another one.
—Irving

The Overnight Book Program is probably the most powerful thing I've ever done in the classroom. It unites the child, the parent, and the teacher in a joyful quest for literacy. It connects with everything we do in the classroom, from reading and writing and art to all other curriculum. It is a vehicle for teaching children how to help each other and how to get help from another child. The program seems complicated to run, but it is really quite simple, as expressed by Irving in the quotation above.

Returning, Talking About, and Choosing Books

When my first graders come into the classroom each morning they put lunches, coats, and backpacks in their cubbies. On their desks they put, from the bottom up, their book bags, booklists, overnight books, and homework. We sometimes call these "book sandwiches." Then they begin reading books from baskets in the center of each team's group of desks.

After I take attendance and wish each child good morning, I can see at a glance if anything is missing. Occasionally I will say, "Hold up your homework. Put it down please. Now hold up your overnight book." If I don't see an overnight book I ask the child about it individually. I put a "B" on my classroom grid (recordkeeping paper for the week) to remind myself to check with the child again the next day. The book almost always comes in after school or the next morning.

It is a disappointing day for the rare child who forgot to return a book: There's no new book to take home today.

Our brief morning reading time is somewhat social. Children browse books from the book baskets or peruse their overnight books. They talk about the books they chose yesterday and will choose today. Some of them try to talk other children out of choosing books that they want to take home themselves.

Team by team, children come up and put their overnight books in the big display rack of bookshelves. They place the books carefully, right side up, with the covers facing out. When all books have been returned, one team at a time (four or five children) comes up to choose new books.

Choosing books is done quickly. Children have been anticipating this moment, and most of them have figured out ahead of time which book they want to take home next. Many of them have also done some negotiating with classmates about this. On the eleventh day of school I heard a child say, with relief and exasperation, "I've been waiting *forever* for this book!"

Children are asked to find out their titles and write them on their booklists. I say, "If you don't know, ask someone to help you." And, "If you *do* know, help somebody puzzle out a word or the title." Those who know where the title is, and know *what* the name of the book is, tell other children. The classroom is a beehive of activity, with children finding out what to write and learning book titles. The atmosphere is something like a game show—except that everyone wins. Children want to find their titles and be able to say them before I call on them. Many repeat the titles over and over as they write the words on their booklists. A few children may go check with another student a second or third time.

I praise some children individually or as a group for helping others. I praise other children for knowing how to go and get help. I want the whole experience to be a positive one and to reflect the class motto, "Here in our classroom we help each other."

One of the major goals of my Overnight Book Program is to help children work together to take responsibility for their learning. I attended a recent business seminar where this question was asked: "What kind of learners do business communities want for the future?" One of the prevalent answers: "People who can work together as part of a problem-solving team." My first graders learn to work together as an integral part of the Overnight Book Program. Being able to get help from each other gives them some strategies for learning that take some of the pressure off "being right" and "knowing."

Children help each other to find the book titles, frame them (put one finger at the beginning of the title and one at the end), write titles down, track words, and hone other skills. They are always at different places in their learning of these skills. This freedom to get help from each other reduces anxiety and gives children a way to proceed. Helping each other gives them interpersonal skills. This emphasis on independence and responsibility builds a strong, functioning learning community. Getting help is not about giving up, but about knowing how to proceed when you can't figure something out.

As children write their titles and tell them to me, I help if necessary, or refer them to a child who will know the title. I speak to children individually: "Oh, good! You know your title!" To a child who has not moved and who cannot

Figure 3–1. Ricky copies a title onto his booklist

remember the book title, I may say, "Find somebody to help you, please." The child does, and soon tells me the title. Often I will ask children to track—point to individual words in the title as they "read" them. I say, "You tracked that title perfectly," or "You can *read* that, you know." As I say this to Irving he smiles smugly and tries not to look too pleased. I notice he has nodded his head. "Aha! I caught him reading!"

Keeping Track of Overnight Books

I have tried many different ways to keep track of books. My latest system, a clipboard with a stack of photocopied class grids, seems to me to be the easiest. Using the computer I create a grid of twenty boxes, one for each child. Each box has a student's name—these are alphabetized—and is large enough to fit a week's worth of book titles. I alternate pen colors day to day. This helps me keep my place if I am interrupted. As I call a child's name and am told the book title, I write it down. I use my own abbreviations and write quickly. It takes a very short time to record all students' book choices. If a book has not come back I circle the title. I know it will come back the next day.

Other ways of keeping track of checked-out books could suit other teachers, depending upon individual goals, student grade levels, and so on. Here is a sampling of other book checkout systems:

Book sign-out forms on a clipboard—grid type. The form lists children's whole names or first names in alphabetical order. Child or teacher writes the book title to sign out the book. This title is crossed out the next day when the book is returned. There could be a separate clipboard of sign-out forms for each team or group of students.

Book sign-out forms on a clipboard—list type. Children's names are listed on the left. Book titles are written on the right. There can be a page a day or one page per week, with abbreviated titles listed. A variation of this is to list book titles on the left and children's names on the right. Books are checked off or crossed out each day when they are returned.

Card check-out. Each book has a pocket and a card with the name of the book on top. Students write their names on the book cards and put the cards into their own personal book pockets on a bulletin board or chart. There is a labeled card pocket for each student.

Sometimes the best way to find the most comfortable organization system is to try out a few and modify them to suit our own teaching styles and goals. I know teachers who assign numbers to books and have students call out the numbers to check out the books. This does not work for my program because I am focused on children learning some reading skills through the book titles. However, such a system may work well for someone with different learning strategies in mind. It really is not necessary that everything be figured out ahead of time before the Overnight Book Program starts. I believe new things must evolve in order to become personalized and work for us.

Dealing with Lost and Damaged Books

Missing books can be a problem and a fear when beginning the book take-home program. I know a missing book will come back because all year long I have stressed the importance of returning books on time. At the beginning of the school year, if a book is missing I will write parents a little note, make a short phone call, or try to speak with parents as they pick up their children after school. I want to let them know that the book did not return and that their child needs to return

Figure 3–2. Book check-out grid

it the next morning. I feel that this is very important. If books are not returned immediately, there is a good chance they will be lost unless the problem is addressed *now*. When I act on the problem right away, everyone involved with the Overnight Book Program—parent, teacher, and child—is aware that the book did not return and *must* be returned the next day.

Occasionally there is a problem: The book has been left at an aunt's house, is riding around in dad's car, and so forth. Once in a great while there is a wait before the book is returned while someone goes to get it at the boy's and girl's club or grandma's house in another city, or looks for it under the bed. The important thing is for everyone involved to know that we are all *waiting* for the book to come back. The child does not take another book home until the missing book has been returned. This is never punitive, just a way to organize that is clear and definite.

Here's a sample of a letter I might send if a book is missing:

Dear Parents,

Yesterday _____ (child's name) took home the book _____ book title) "for overnight." I hope that everyone in the family enjoyed the book.

Unfortunately the book did not come back to school today.

Would you please help _____(child's name) look for the book and return it to school in the morning? Another child is waiting for the book.

Thank you very much for your help in keeping our overnight book library intact.

Sincerely,

_____(Your child's teacher)

If a parent wishes to pay for a lost book, I recommend waiting for a short time to be sure that the book is not found. I try to sympathize and suggest places to look for it. Most of the time the book shows up within the week. If a book does seem to be lost forever I ask the parent to pay the approximate cost to replace it. I buy the replacement copy immediately. When the replaced book is put on the display rack we all celebrate the return of this title to our classroom overnight book library.

I really must stress that books have been lost or damaged *very* few times in the more than twenty-three years I have had an Overnight Book Program.

Occasionally you may see a look of anxiety on the face of a child during book-choosing time. This happened once for two or three days before I figured out the cause, since the child did not seem to want to talk. All became clear when Favi chose a book—a new one—and found marking pen writing *all* over it. Fortunately, she showed me the book. I checked the record on my clipboard and found the name of the last person who had taken the book home. After a little private talk, Kenny told me that "the little kid at his house wrote all over the book." Knowing that Kenny was an only child, I understood exactly why he had seemed anxious. We had another chat, which included Kenny's mother, and the book was paid for and replaced. Kenny took the damaged book home. I mention this incident because it illustrates the importance of keeping an accurate book checkout record.

Creating a Book Collection

When I was setting up my Overnight Book Program I went to library sales and purchased books for twenty-five and fifty cents. I went to garage sales and flea markets and children's bookstores. I chose quality literature books in good condition. I bought paperback books from school book clubs and some new hardback books from children's bookstores. I continued to study and read and work to increase my ability to choose good literature.

There are many publications for help in choosing quality books for children. Among them are *The Horn Book Magazine*, *The Horn Book Guide*, *Book Links*, *School Library Journal*, and such books as *Valerie and Walter's Best Books for Children—A Lively and Opinionated Guide*, by Valerie V. Lewis and Walter M. Mayes. See the bibliography for other recommendations.

Getting book recommendations from teachers whose opinions you value is also helpful. It has been invaluable to me to have Kay Goines as a resource, mentor, and friend for most of my teaching career.

Professional development classes and workshops in children's literature are available through most colleges and universities. Many universities have extension courses for teachers. County reading associations and some bookstores also hold programs in children's literature.

Teachers can all use funds to help implement an Overnight Book Program. One way to get money for books for the classroom is to write a grant. Grant information is usually disseminated through state, county, and district offices of education at the beginning of each school year.

Borrowing Books for the Program

At the beginning of my Overnight Book Program I spoke with librarians in the city where I teach and discovered that I could borrow from forty to sixty books at a time for a six-week time period with a teacher library card. I did this for a while until I built up my own book collection. The library was a wonderful resource, but there were some drawbacks to borrowing in quantity. It took a lot of heavy lifting to borrow that many books. Keeping track of them all was difficult. I finally noticed that my first graders were hiding their favorite books so that I could not find them to take them back to the library. Every four to six weeks I had my own personal scavenger hunt! Borrowing fewer books and purchasing some of the favorites seemed to be a better solution for me. However, I always use the public library. I check out the new books as they come in each season to try them out in my classroom before purchasing any. This helps me avoid purchasing books—even those with wonderful reviews—that just do not work in my classroom.

I also use the school library, checking out books weekly when the children do. Sometimes I can arrange to keep a few books in the classroom for a longer time period. I use these as part of the Overnight Book Program, but I always record with extra care the name of the child who has taken the book home.

Offering Book Choices

I soon realized that I needed only one book per child and a few extras to begin the Overnight Book Program. Working with fewer take-home books at the beginning of the program gave the children *more* opportunities to learn. I kept a multitude of additional books in the classroom on other bookshelves, in a big red wagon, in baskets, and in tubs, much as I do now.

I feel strongly that children need a variety of books: some older library editions, some new hardbacks and paperbacks, book club editions, and so forth. It is important that children be exposed to the best literature available, and that the books all be in good repair. An advantage to library book-sale books is that they already have plastic book covers when I purchase them. Other new hardback books need to be outfitted with plastic covers before they go home with children.

Getting Books Ready to Send Home

I purchase book-cover plastic on twelve-inch rolls from Gaylord Bros. (see Appendix 2). I take off the book jacket and cut the plastic to fit it. I insert the book jacket in the plastic sleeve and tape the plastic-covered book jacket to the book. If a book is smaller than twelve inches the plastic can be folded to fit and then taped in place on the inside of the cover. One twelve-inch roll of plastic for a school site is a good way to begin protecting books. Examining a public library book will help these instructions become clear.

An alternative to plastic book covers is to laminate book covers and tape them to the books. Strapping tape is the strongest tape to use to attach either laminated or plastic-covered book covers to the books.

I discovered that paperback books last longer when I use clear wide packaging tape on the inside front and back covers. I run a strip of tape to adhere the front and back covers to the adjoining book pages. This keeps the cover from falling off and the book from falling apart. I also put a piece of tape on the spine of the book. I put a line of tape all around the inside front and back covers.

Another way to prolong the life of paperbacks is to cover them with clear stick-on plastic, also called laminating paper. Books are such an investment that it is worth the time to cover them and reinforce them so they will last and last.

Occasionally I take a glue gun to a book to glue a hardcover back on or do a major repair. A low-melt type glue gun is safe for teacher use in the classroom.

You may wish to obtain parent help with the task of keeping books covered, taped, and in good condition. Sometimes I have this kind of support, sometimes I do not. I am still able to run my Overnight Book Program myself. Parent help is wonderful but not crucial.

Teaching Children About Book Care

At the beginning of the school year many children are just learning how to handle books—how to hold them and how to turn pages—and general book care. This is a good reason for using older well-loved books at this time of year. When children get new hardback book choices later on, they will have already practiced and learned book handling. Starting with older books will also make things easier on your nerves if you are new to sending your own precious books home with your students!

In my classroom we talk a great deal about how to take care of books. I occasionally tell the children that the books "talk" about them when they are not at school. "Somebody's book was really upset after school today," I say. "It was complaining and complaining, and yelling 'My child *pinched* me!' "

"What did my book say?" they all ask excitedly. "Hmm, I'm not sure," I reply, pausing as if trying to remember specifics. "I think your book was the one that said, 'My child knows how to turn the pages. It didn't hurt a bit, and I'm not all wrinkled!' "

We also talk about what the classroom animals—several large bears, a gigantic lion, and many smaller stuffed animals—do while they read our books at night. Many minor tears and small damages are attributed to these "classroom critters," who may also be blamed when things are misplaced or not put back correctly. This reinforces book and materials care and organization without placing blame on specific children. It relieves the pressure of having to do everything perfectly when children believe that animals that have been in the classroom for years still make mistakes.

Using a Weekly Newsletter

As part of my goal to keep the Overnight Book Program running smoothly, I send a weekly newsletter that informs parents whether books are being returned on time. The *Braggin' Dragan* goes home with my students each Friday. The newsletter gives highlights of the week in each subject area, lists of titles of books we have particularly enjoyed, the words to a poem we are learning, and notice of any upcoming events. It also includes brief circled student evaluations numbered one (fantastic!) to five (really needs improvement). The areas evaluated are "Listens and follows directions— works hard to learn," "Gets along well with others," and "Returns books and homework on time." There is a small space for comments and space for parent signatures and optional responses. I use this evaluation area if a book is missing or was not returned on time. I also try to write a brief positive comment on top of each child's newsletter.

I keep a classroom grid for each week with brief notes in order to fill out this newsletter accurately. For example, "B" in a square of the weekly classroom grid would mean that a book was not returned on time. (After two "B's" I would have made a phone call or sent a note to parents.) "H" means "homework missing," "A" means "aggressive behavior," and so forth. I invent new codes as the need arises.

I jot brief anecdotal notes in another grid weekly, and date and save these. They give me at a glance an overview of what is going on in the classroom with each child every week. The intent of the newsletter is to keep parents in the know. The classroom grids also keep *me* in the know over time. I tape them into my grade book each week for future reference. And the *Braggin' Dragan* newsletter helps keep the overnight books coming back each day.

Sometimes I receive wonderful comments on the bottom of the returned newsletters. Those I particularly treasure describe a child's love of reading and growing abilities in literacy.

These newsletters also help with parent questions and concerns, and give me another way to measure how things seem to be going in our quest to learn.

4

Fostering Successful Literacy

A book is special to me. It helps me to read.
—Jenna

Our classroom is infused with energy and excitement. Children move to sit in a circle on the rug with newly chosen overnight books in front of them. We have just enjoyed reading a "big book" together and acted out a favorite poem. Now we are all set to have a variety of learning experiences focusing on the overnight books children picked today.

Playing Literacy Games and Other Activites

Some children flip pages, perusing their books. Others move to let someone else fit in the circle, or to ask a question of a friend. "Frame your book title with two fingers," I say. "Now count the words in your title. Check children near you and see if they need help." It is early in the school year, but most children can now frame their titles. A few scramble to get help from a friend, then come back to the book circle. "Thumbs up if you have three words in your title," I say. Several children put up thumbs. They can all read their three-word book titles. I ask children to raise their hands if their title begins like "mouse" or "Mom." We have winners here, too.

Now it's time for a comprehension-type riddle: "Stand up if the character in your story gets in trouble, gets sent to his room, and then has a great adventure." The children know that this *has* to be Max from the book *Where the Wild Things Are*. Hugo knows too and stands up. He reads the title and points to the words. Hugo is thrilled that he can read, and so am I.

These games we play are a bit like a literary Simon Says, except no one is "out." Everybody *gets* involved and everybody *stays* involved.

I like to start with these simple games each day and build to more challenging ones. Every day we have questions of varying degrees of type and complexity. We just see where the books, titles, and stories take us on our literary journey.

Part of the success of this activity is that it is short. And it is always different. Some days we check book titles to see if there are "word-wall" words, words that begin like "chew" and "church," titles about animals, titles about songs and games, titles that answer story comprehension questions. Everything is spontaneous, dependent upon which overnight books have been chosen that day. The children are learning to use phonics, memory of story text, and other reading strategies *in the context of reading.*

I make riddles and ask questions, and so do the children. It is important that *they* ask questions. Their riddles get trickier as their vocabularies increase. Their attention spans increase too. "Find a book about working with your buddy," I say. "*Officer Buckle and Gloria,*" says Jenna. She easily shows me which word is "Gloria." She says, "This is the book that makes us laugh the most." Other children agree.

Some days we open books and have scavenger hunts, finding specific words, words that begin with, end with, rhyme with, and so forth. The pace is relaxed. Children like making suggestions for words to find and for questions to ask about the stories. We have heard all these stories read aloud, but we gain more familiarity with the text through these games. We notice similarities between books and say, "Oh, *The Three Little Javalinas* is like *The Three Little Pigs!*" Or, "George and Martha are friends like Frog and Toad are friends!" Francisco says he is going to write a story about Danny and the dinosaur "bein' in an adventure" with Curious George. We all think that is a great idea. Several children have suggestions for him. We are having fun making connections, and the children are learning.

Another day I tell the children how excited I am about all the words they know. "See how many words you can read that you didn't even *know* you can read!" I say. I hold up a tagboard sentence strip with a book title printed on it. The children are astonished to see that they know what it says. They read several book-title sentence strips. They find they can match the strips to books. Children just can't believe they know all these words. It is a thrilling moment for us all. They are *really* reading! Another day I cut up the book titles and the children read individual words. Using a pocket chart, they put words together to form titles, then find the matching book. This becomes a literacy center activity they enjoy.

Some days we think of categories of books. The children come up with "funny books," "books about special people we like," "books about things that go," "books about animals." We find a large paper for each category and a few children copy our category titles onto charts.

To "play categories," children write their favorite titles on sentence strips. They match these strips to the category where they feel the book belongs. This game is played with the large group or in small groups in literacy centers.

Figure 4–1. "Playing categories" with category charts

Sometimes children glue the sentence strips on the category charts and illustrate the charts. We enjoy looking at these. We read the book titles and think of other categories, and other books that could go in those categories.

On other days we play a variation of Kay Goines' "literary game," an activity she developed using excerpts chosen from favorite stories and poems. I have made a set of excerpts and glued each one on a six-by-eight-inch card. To start the game I recite an excerpt from a story, poem, or nursery rhyme. The children wait until I have finished and then say the title and author's name. Other times I say the title or author's name and children recite the excerpt. For example, if I say "Hundreds of cats, thousands of cats, millions and billions and trillions of cats," the children join in reciting the excerpt if they know it. Then they wait to be called on to say, "*Millions of Cats* by Wanda Gag." When we play the literary game there is a lot of anticipation and a lot of learning!

Working in Book Circles

The children are passionate about these books and stories—they like to read and interact with them. They like using them to play the games: to find letters, sounds, words, answer comprehension questions, make up their own questions and riddles, recite book excerpts, and tell authors' names and titles. When we do book circle activities everyone succeeds, everyone helps someone else. All the children are engaged. We end by celebrating, discussing all our good ideas. The book circle provides a forum, a place for all our remarks, comments, and observations about books. The magical part is that these words we read *mean* something to us all. We practice "book talk" as a group, and children learn to talk about books with each other, in small groups, or with partners.

It is best to have a mixture of activities each day during book circle so that all children are challenged and all of them can have success. My school has a specific phonics program. I always double-check and see what parts of it I can cover or emphasize using the books and stories we enjoy. Sometimes I do short phonics mini-lessons focused on the overnight books. For example, I may notice that three or four of the books chosen have words with the "ight" sound. I'll review the sound on the whiteboard and the children will look for it in words in their titles or in the stories. Children *do* learn a lot more phonics in the context of reading. And they *love* the thrill of the hunt!

During book circle time the emphasis is not just on phonics, it is on all reading strategies. And most of all, it is on the *meaning* of the words, stories, and books we enjoy. Hopefully, these types of activities will whet children's appetites for reading. When children *want* to read they are more apt to learn. And when children get the chance to ask questions, they "buy into" the idea of books having meaning to think about. This idea empowers them and helps them get on the road to learning.

Questions and riddles during book circle time can relate to letter recognition, phonemic awareness, phonics, rhyming words, long and short vowels, blends, digraphs, and phonemes. They can also relate to the elements of story: character, plot, setting, sequence, concepts, themes, genre, and so forth. Questions can also pertain to illustrations: their style and media, and looking at pictures for a sense of the story. Questions can elicit story quotes, poetry, titles, and the names of authors and illustrators.

Here are some of the questions and activities I use during book circle time. I mix them up to vary our focus and use only a few questions each day.

- Frame the title with two fingers, one on each side of the title.
- Track the words in the title, pointing to each word as it is said. Count

the words in the title. (This helps children understand one-to-one correspondence.)

- Find the word I am segmenting: *all-i-ga-tors*.
- Find the letter _____.
- Find a word that begins with _____.
- Find a word that ends with _____.
- Find a word with two syllables.
- Find a long-vowel word.
- Find a short-vowel word.
- Find a word with two vowels together where the first vowel "talks."
- Find a word that rhymes with _____.
- Find a book title that has rhyming words.
- Find a root word.
- Find a long-vowel word with a magic "e" at the end.
- Find the sound you hear at the beginning of _____.

Questions can address genre, illustrations, and mood:

- Find a fairy tale.
- Find a book of nursery rhymes or poetry.
- Find a book about numbers.
- Find an alphabet book.
- Find a book about shapes and colors.
- Which book has a plot like *Red Riding Hood* (or another familiar story)?
- Find the book with photographs for illustrations.
- Find a poetry book.
- Find the book with illustrations in a border that tells more about the story.
- Find a book with a scary mood.

Some questions can be much more personal and lead to good literature discussions:

- Find a book with a character you would love to meet.
- Is there a book with a setting you would like to live in?
- Find the book with an adventure you would love to have.
- Find a book with an art style you wish to try out.
- Is there a book with an author you particularly admire?
- Is there a book you would like to hear or read again and again and again? Do you know why?
- Find a book that makes you laugh.
- Is there a book with illustrations that are special for you?
- Find the book with the character who . . .

- Find the book that's set in . . .
- Find the book where . . .
- What questions would *you* like to ask about a book?

With these types of questions children need time for discussion, time to explain their thinking, and time to talk about the books.

The emphasis is not on right or wrong answers in these games, but on the thrill of discovery, making connections, finding out, and enjoying books and stories. In doing these activities together we learn and talk and connect things in ways we never would have dreamed. Some days we have very loose and creative brainstorming sessions about books. The more children talk about books, the more they notice—and the more their thinking is stimulated and extended.

Poetry Cubes

Some days in our book circle we use the "poetry cube," which is closely related to the literary game. We have a variety of cubes, large and small, some made from two half-gallon milk cartons cut to cube size and put together. (See Appendix 4 for details about making poetry cubes.)

The favorite cube near the beginning of the year is quite large, made from our computer printer box. It was taped closed and covered with butcher paper like a present, then a large illustrated poem was taped on each cube "face." The poems were chosen favorites of the children. One child illustrated each poem. We will change poems or book excerpts soon, or perhaps we will use a different cube.

Sometimes the children build with the cubes, reading the poetry and book excerpts as they stack them and create forms, sculptures, totem poles, forts, walls, castles, houses, and so on. In one activity, a child gets up to roll the cube. There is anticipation because the poem that lands face-up is the one we will say together. The cube roller chooses another child to read the poem. This particular child knows the poem well and prefers to say it first alone, while tracking text with a finger. Then the group recites the poem with gusto. The child who read now chooses someone else to roll the cube.

Some days when it is time for a new cube, children sit together on the rug with piles of favorite books. This time we will be making a "book excerpt cube." Children browse through books avidly, looking for the part they like best, the words that express the heart of the book. We choose six favorite book excerpts. (Others can be saved for future use or other projects.) The excerpts are written or printed in large type onto nine-by-twelve-inch white or light-colored construction paper. A child illustrates each excerpt, then we affix the excerpts to the cube faces with Fun-Tak Reusable Adhesive or tape rolls (pieces of tape rolled backward, sticky side up). These book excerpts may be removed when we remake

Figure 4–2. Marek rolls the poetry cube

the cube—when we move on to other books that we love to quote. Or we may decide to keep this cube and add it to our collection.

Building Blocks

My first graders like to use our set of wooden building blocks to stack and construct all kinds of forms and structures. It seemed a shame to let a reading opportunity go by, so I have begun taping large-type poetry and book excerpts to each block. I use tape rolls to affix a poem to each side of a block, then cover the side with clear adhesive paper or wide wrapping tape. I reserve the narrow ends of the blocks for alphabet letters or children's names. I don't want to say that the children are skill building, but that *is* my intent! They can read, chant, sing, and discover as they create forms with the blocks. Reading these poems and excerpts and songs is just left to happen at whim with an emphasis on discovery and fun.

Creative Dramatics

Some days in the book circle children choose to enact a book they love. A frequent favorite choice is *Pierre* by Maurice Sendak. They all love Pierre because he always says, "I don't care!" We talk about how maybe this is not such a great sentence to use at home. We "play" with it in school instead.

Children sit in a circle on the rug or on the edges of the U-shaped team desks. We all say as many parts of the book as we can—together. I move my arms as if I am conducting an orchestra and say *"Pierre*—Chapter One!" We all announce the chapters this way.

I sit back at the edge of the book circle. I tell the children playing the characters some of the words to repeat, or they come up with them. The "audience"—the children not enacting one of the parts—also chimes in. The child taking the part of Pierre may really ham it up, and we eat it up! We don't worry about knowing lines—actors have complete freedom to play their parts. When Francisco plays Pierre he always gives himself an invisible "TV remote control" that he holds and plays with as he ignores his parents and shouts, "I don't care!"

The audience participation in this activity is very important. The audience is made up of our class only and all the children have the freedom to recite the words to the story as they remember it. This is a wonderful chance for *all* the children to "choral perform," not just the four or five who enact the play. This year I found that Brenda, who always chose *not* to play the part of a character, knew the entire book by heart and could recite all of it with great enthusiasm. I learned this only because I sat on a desk next to her while I was "conducting" the play.

The last day of school this year we enacted *Pierre* about five times, with different "casts," and it still wasn't enough. Some children really did not want to leave. Like Pierre, at the end of the story, they *did care*.

Poetry Charts and Cracking the Code

I touched on poetry charts in Chapter 1 when I described the nursery rhyme activity we do for *Humpty Dumpty* on the first day of school. Poetry charts are an ongoing class activity that always begins with an oral language experience. We learn a poem, recite it, chant it, act it, mime it, dance and sing and love it. Then the words to the poem mysteriously appear on a large piece of twenty-four-by-thirty-six-inch oak tag chart paper. I never tell the children what these words are—that would be taking their discoveries away from them. It is always a very exciting moment when the code is cracked and it becomes clear to the children what the words on the chart say.

I feel that I am witnessing a miracle when I see children crack the code and find meaning in formerly inexplicable marks and symbols. I try to convey the mystery of this to my first graders. I tell the children about the Rosetta stone, found in Egypt about two hundred years ago. For many years no one could decode it. Knowledge of how to read Egyptian hieroglyphs had been lost for almost three thousand years. Then, after years of study and trial and error, Jean-Francois Champollion "cracked the code," making many things about life in ancient Egypt clear. For first graders' purposes it is not necessary to know names and dates. I want them to have a feeling about other people discovering knowledge throughout time, throughout history, just as they themselves will do in first grade and throughout their lives. For teacher reference, however, I recommend *The Riddle of the Rosetta Stone: Key to Ancient Egypt* by James Cross Giblin.

Pointers

When children have uncovered the hidden meaning of the poetry chart that suddenly appeared on our classroom wall we double-check by reading it together. One of the best ways for us to read a "big book," a piece of writing on an overhead projector, or a large chart as a group is with a pointer. I use the pointer first and point to each word as we say the poem. Later I may let children point to the words, taking turns being the pointer for the group. Pointers help us to focus on individual words, follow the direction of the print, keep the place, and stay together as we choral read.

Pointers are handy and can be fun and creative. There are many types. It is much more interesting to use a pointer if the class has a collection of them. Some pointer ideas are chopsticks, colored dowels from an art supply store, and decorative garden items such as a pointed stick with a bird carved on top. Many companies now make teacher products and have pointers with different animals or story characters on the handles. I have pointers with an apple handle, a giraffe, an elephant, parrots, and a tiger. One pointer is a clean flyswatter with a rectangle cut out of the center, used for finding one word at a time—the selected word shows through the cut-out space.

Other places to look for pointers are inexpensive import-export stores and stationery stores. You can also make your own pointers with small wooden toys, dowels, and a glue gun. Decorative pencils with fancy erasers are also fun to use for pointers—just don't sharpen the pencil. Of course, fingers are perfect pointers too!

Illustrating Poetry Charts

I use many ways of illustrating poetry charts in the classroom. Sometimes parents are interested in illustrating them at home, either by themselves or with their children. I send home the rolled-up poem and some materials, such as marking pens, crayons, and watercolor paints. Other times, everyone in the class illustrates a chart. The drawings are cut out and affixed to the chart.

Individual children sometimes illustrate a poetry chart. A small group of children will work together to do the drawings for one chart. Occasionally I have several poetry charts ready to be illustrated and the class as a whole divides into groups to illustrate them.

Children's art on the poetry charts translates the text and gives us beautiful illustrations to enjoy. Children learn that they must understand the text clearly if they are to illustrate it accurately. We enjoy both the process of creating the art on the charts, and the finished charts themselves.

Murals

Once in a while a poetry chart turns into a mural, as described in Chapter 1 with our torn-paper mural for *Millions of Cats*. To make murals, children can illustrate right on colored non-fading paper with oil pastels or tempera paint. Often small groups of children create backgrounds this way. Students can also illustrate on other papers, then cut out their drawings and glue them to the mural later. It is easier to control things when drawings are glued on after all the art is complete. The selected poem or book excerpt can be typed or handwritten and glued on by the teacher. Then the completed illustrations are added to illuminate the words we have chosen. We do not glue anything on the mural until we move things around several times and decide on the composition. Then we spend a lot of time talking about what we have created. This talk is called *aesthetic valuing*. For more information on aesthetic valuing, see the *Visual and Performing Arts Framework for California Public Schools, Kindergarten Through Grade Twelve*.

Media for Poetry Charts and Murals I prefer using crayon and marking-pen drawings early in the school year. I also like to start the children doing torn-paper art right away, before they become dependent on scissors. Later in the year children are able to handle oil pastels, which yield very bright, intense colors. They smear a little, but not as much as chalk. They are very satisfying for children.

An easy way to add lively, interesting background color to a poetry chart or mural is to use shaving cream and food coloring. Just squirt a "poof" of shaving cream about the size of a large fist onto a paper plate. Drip two or three drops of each color food coloring onto the mound of shaving cream. It is not even necessary to mix the food coloring in: Just take a three-by-five card or folded piece of construction paper and *scrape* the shaving cream and color over a crayon drawing or *around* a marking-pen drawing (pen will smear when wet). Make sure the shaving cream is all scraped and absorbed, with no remaining residue. Half the fun of this is that you never know what effect you are going to get. The shaving cream and food coloring mixture dries almost instantly.

An alternative to food coloring is to mix shaving cream with a slight bit of tempera paint. This also needs to be scraped across paper with cardstock. It too dries almost instantly. It is fast and easy. Another product that can be added to shaving cream is liquid watercolor (see Appendix 2). Food coloring and liquid watercolor mix with shaving cream to add bright clear transparent color to a chart. The shaving-cream-and-tempera mixture yields a more opaque, creamy color.

It is important to get a brand of shaving cream with a pleasing aroma, because the smell will be noticeable in the classroom. Avoid menthol brands as they make fingers slightly numb. One paper plate with shaving cream is more than enough for a group of four or five children, and enough for one poetry chart.

Problem-Solving with Literacy Experiences

Mike Mulligan and His Steam Shovel, written by Virginia Lee Burton in 1940, is a literary classic. It is the story of a steam shovel that gets stuck in the cellar it digs for the town hall of Popperville. Will Mary Anne, the steam shovel, be able to get out of the hole? Will Mike Mulligan, the steam shovel operator, and Mary Anne be able to complete the job on time? (If not, there will be no payment.) What will happen? What is the best way to solve this problem?

I do not complete the reading of the book. I stop when I get to the problem about what Mike and Mary Anne will do. The children have many different, interesting solutions. We discuss them and mull them over. Stopping the reading at this point is my idea, but they are very interested in talking about this problem and do not seem to want to resume the reading yet.

Hugo says, "They hafta get a string and the people can get strings and pull." Jenna's idea is that "They might take Mary Anne apart." Sara is in favor of everybody—Mike Mulligan and Mary Anne—climbing out on a ladder, but Francisco says, "They can get a piece of wood and get up it." Edgar agrees, but expresses this his own way: "They could find a rectangle board and put it down to the cellar. Then the man could get out with the steam truck."

This whole discussion and the depth of the children's concern and their problem-solving abilities fascinate me. They are totally involved. They stretch their vocabularies and extend their ways of thinking to come up with solutions. The children draw the problem and solution, and write their own text. They also dictate their responses to me to type on the computer and use on a literacy chart. They cannot get enough of the book. During centers a small group of children spontaneously use big blocks, toy figures, and a wooden crane I didn't even

How Did Mike Mulligan and
Mary Anne Get Out of the Cellar? Haneen

They can mak a
bigbighoole to
getowt.

Figure 4–3. Haneen's solution to the steam shovel's problem

remember we had to test out and modify their ideas. We can all visualize the magnitude of the problem much more clearly when we look at and talk about the children's model of the steam shovel in the cellar.

The creative activity grew out of the children's interest—their passion—and their curiosity.

Later that day we finish the book.

5

Imaging the Story

The place where the story is, I always think I'm there.
—Edgar

Experiencing the Power of Story with Sustained Silent Reading

It is time for sustained silent reading, or "DEAR time," in my classroom. My first graders and I all "drop everything and read" during these fifteen (later on, twenty-plus) minutes of the day. It is a time for children to practice their reading strategies and skills, to practice being readers, to learn to *love* to read. Sometimes we call this time our "reading present." This regularly structured time for reading each day helps children develop the habit of reading and value the time they spend this way.

The children have all chosen a book and are engaged in varying degrees. Some are looking at pictures. Others are trying to make sense of the text and illustrations. Some children, like Edgar and Haneen, are really reading and have mentally gone right inside the books, to visualize and experience the stories and meander in the pages. Other children fidget and look around to find someone to talk to. The instructions were explicit: "We have a fifteen-minute 'reading present.' Have a great time with your book. And of course no one bothers anyone else. . . ." I ask the children not to talk to each other, not to distract each other, because they might keep someone from "falling inside the book and really reading!" We start with five or seven minutes, increasing the time to longer but still comfortable periods as the year progresses.

I want all these children to read whenever they have a chance, and to *believe* they are readers. I tell them about the day when *I* became a reader. It was winter. It was cold and dark and I could not go outside and play. I remember feeling very bored. Everyone in my family was busy except for me. My brother and sister were doing something together and my father and mother were reading. "Why don't you read?" my Mother asked, after listening to me complain and fuss.

I did have a book nearby. It was big and thick and had no pictures except for the one on the cover. I really did love that picture on the cover, and I looked at it for a long time. I opened the book. I started looking at the words, then looked around the living room—still no action there. I looked at the words again and read a few. I read a few more. I began to get a picture in my head of what was happening in the story. I turned the page. I read and read and read. When I looked up I was surprised to see that I was still in the living room. My mind was still inside the story. And when I looked I saw that I was on page thirty-eight! I had looked at books before. But this time the book *took* me somewhere—the little marks on the page had changed into a whole and real other world, and I had been swooped right into it!

What I discovered on that wintry evening, all by myself, is that story has the power to take us out of ourselves, then return us to where we were. And sometimes, if we read a book that really speaks to us, we are not the same when we return. Some part of us is changed forever.

I tell my first graders how excited and mystified I was by this whole experience. I could not believe I read a few words, and then more, and felt as if I had been far, far away inside a story. I kept thinking that if my parents had not been busy reading themselves and my brother and sister had not been occupied, I would have missed this whole experience!

For me, being able to *visualize* the story was what made the experience so powerful and real. It is fascinating to see children acquire this ability. Many, like Edgar, are excited about it and try to express it. The experience holds mystery and power for him, as it always has for me.

Combining sustained silent reading with the Overnight Book Program gives children a greater chance of having reading experiences where they can visualize what is happening and go right down deep inside a book and live in the author's imaginary world. During our "reading present" activity, children have *time* with books they have chosen themselves. They have the memory of the text, from having heard the story. Hopefully they have visualizations from the read-aloud experience that will also help them on their journey to decoding the text themselves. The amazing thing is not that children can "crack the code" and can "read" the words. The miracle for me is that those words and the images they evoke can carry children lands and worlds away, to other times and places, to have other experiences and to meet people and characters they would never have known.

Modeling Reading Strategies

During sustained silent reading I usually put myself in the children's places because then I can most honestly see and feel what they are experiencing. The best way for me to do this is to read something that's difficult for me, so I usually read novels or picture books in Spanish. I explain to the children that this reading is a little hard for me, but I always feel good about doing it. I can feel my reading improving and I can increasingly visualize the story in my mind. I relay to them parts of the story that I enjoy. I tell them truthfully that if I read in Spanish every day it is much easier. If I skip even two or three days it is harder for me to get into the book.

Once in a while I read aloud to the children from a bilingual Spanish-English picture book. The children who do not know Spanish get the gist of the story from the English translation. Those who do not speak English or Spanish get the idea from the pictures. As the story progresses I say things like, "Oh, do you hear how much better I sound now after just that little bit of practice!" Of course they agree! On different days I explain strategies I use to figure out words or ideas. One day a child said, in astonishment, "Ohhhh! You do just what *we* hafta do!"

One time I was most gratified because I had indeed practiced before class the reading of Alma Flor Ada's English and Spanish picture book *The Lizard and the Sun/La lagartija y el sol.* As I read aloud to my first graders I felt a new strength and ability in my reading. The children noticed it too and were quite proud of me. "Oh, teacher, you did *well!*" said Frankie. Many of the children nodded their heads. "Very impressive," said Maggie. Everyone agreed. Never have I felt so complimented!

This and similar incidents help the children believe that if they work on something they want to learn, success is indeed within their grasp. When they see me struggling and improving, they are more confident of their own ultimate success. I use these techniques to help children see into my thinking, see the ways I puzzle things out when I truly do not know.

Helping Children Learn to Visualize

When I read aloud to children, as I do several times each day, I make sure that one of the books I read has few or no illustrations. Novels or chapter books that are above the children's reading level or folk or fairy tales work well for this activity. This *listening* experience gives children time and practice for making their own mental pictures, for visualizing what is happening in the story.

One type of follow-up to listening to a story is to give children time to elaborate on their own story images by drawing them or combining pictures, words, phrases, and sentences. Sometimes the children draw or write at their desks as they are listening. Other times they do so after the read-aloud experience. I prefer to have our "community of readers" together during the reading of a story and give them time after the book has been read. However the time is planned, this activity enables children to access their own visualizations and imaginings and put them down in more concrete form.

These responses are "thinking maps," or "story maps," that show story details, sequence, characters, setting, action, and relevant words and phrases. They may be word-and-picture doodles. The emphasis is not on neatness or accuracy, but on a chance for children to imagine, visualize, re-image—and to see where their own pictures, words, and phrases about the story take them.

Connecting Art and Writing

I want to blur the line between drawing and writing. Drawing can help propel children into writing, and help them over the beginning-to-write hump. For a few children, those who Howard Gardner, author of several books about multiple intelligences, would identify as having visual/spatial intelligence, this combination of drawing and writing may continue to be a way of looking at the world, a preferred method of self-expression.

After lunch we have sustained silent reading. After recess, for approximately five to seven minutes, we have sustained silent drawing. This short activity focuses on drawing, on looking to "see," and on any language and literacy connections the child wishes to make. Another good time for sustained silent drawing is a ten-minute block of time just before going home.

Sustained Silent Drawing

I have made each child a sketchbook from ten sheets of twelve-by-eighteen-inch white drawing paper. I fold the papers, add a colored construction paper cover, and staple them. Children love having sketchbooks. They put the date (our secret code, i.e., 9/18) on top of the new page. I usually create a new set-up for the children to draw each day. Occasionally the same set-up is used for two or more days. Children may draw this set-up, complete a previous drawing, or draw something else they can see in the classroom. If they prefer, they may make an imaginative drawing. If they wish to include writing or make thinking or story maps, they are free to do so.

The set-up usually takes seconds: I put a pumpkin on top of the tall red stool, or we focus on a vase of flowers brought by a student. We may draw stuffed animals or toys, or make a still life of them by arranging them quickly in a grouping. Other times the children draw and model for each other. As the year progresses I try to make the set-ups a little more complex. For example, if two children want to model for the group, I may pose one slightly behind another so that the artists can learn about overlapping things in their drawings. Children have a lot of in-put creating scenes or compositions to draw.

I explain to the children that our brains are complex and do many jobs. I tell them that the half of our brain that specializes in talking is a different side than the half that controls drawing. I tell them that their drawings will be better, that they will really be able to get into the drawing process, if they are not talking when they are making pictures.

We are fast when we draw. I usually model the process by drawing, but I do not share my work, except for an occasional beginning line or two. Sometimes I suggest media: pencil or crayon or marking pen, a combination of those, or free choice. After five to seven minutes we stop. If the children choose to share their work they leave sketchbooks open on their desks. Otherwise, they just close their sketchbooks and put them away. We take a one-minute walk-through and look at student work—and of course there are no negative comments. Children may work on these drawings again during free time, centers, or the next day's sustained silent drawing time. Like sustained silent reading, this activity helps children learn important habits: reading and drawing.

Sketching Book Images

One year, after admiring a "literature character" mural painted at the school en-trance, my first graders sat down outside to sketch their favorite book characters. They drew in their sketchbooks, intent on their task. A colleague later told me that the upper-grade teachers were watching from the faculty room window.

"Look how cute they are!" one teacher said. "They almost look like they know what they are doing!" At the end of recess this teacher walked past to look at the children's sketches. "They *do* know what they're doing!" she said to a colleague in astonishment.

Children can accomplish a great deal when they have knowledge of strate-gies and techniques, time to practice, and belief in themselves. For these first graders, sketching had become an ordinary, everyday experience, a habit—not something to be feared or avoided. The children learned to carry this new skill over to their free time as a matter of course. As Michael, one of my first graders, expressed it one day, "Me and my grandpa went up to Sign Hill on Saturday and I sketched the mountain."

I make several sketchbooks for each child in the course of a year. These sketch-books are saved in children's portfolios and are important and very illuminating assessment tools for viewing a child's progress, interests, and feelings. They can be used at parent conferences to show the child's growth and development. They are especially helpful in meetings about possible special education placements.

Children love to look through their own collections of sketchbooks. Often a child will deny having done a specific beginning-of-the-year drawing. Other children say things like, "Oh, this was before I could draw really good." Children love the memories their sketches evoke.

Sometimes when children are enamored of a particular book we take more time for story responses of all kinds. This year's class loves to model a pose from a book—their idea! A current favorite is *Pierre* by Maurice Sendak. Typically one child poses as Pierre in an "I don't care!" pose. One to four other characters—mother, father, lion, doctor—pose appropriately and the "scene" is quickly drawn.

Another way we respond to literature through art is to make a still life that represents the book. Children can work in a group or individually, making parts of the story: the characters, things to show the setting, and so forth. Stuffed animals may be used. This final tableau is set up on a cardboard box or stool, and the children draw it. Sometimes the scene is put in the center of the rug and children sit on the rug to draw.

Usually when we do this activity the books we use are overnight books, because everyone has heard them and most children have taken them home. This drawing activity may be given more time, as children usually have a lot of interest in and energy for it. With some children it also evolves into a writing activity, or is something they write about during writer's workshop.

A lot of discussion grows out of our still life set-up activities as well as the follow-up drawing times. Children pool their knowledge, visualizing the story, the text, and the illustrations. They work together to create a common scene. They are stretching their abilities to visualize, and to communicate and share ideas. Often they add words, sentences, or their own stories—as well as drawings—to their sketchbooks and work on them for days.

A recent example of this kind of activity occurred when my first graders decided they wanted to draw *The Shopping Basket* by John Burningham. There are a number of animal characters in this story, and different stuffed animals represented them: a "nasty" dog, an elephant, a monkey, and so forth. The main character, a child, was quickly drawn and cut out by one student and affixed to a paper roll so it would stand up. Someone else made the mother and another child the same way. Children worked together to fix the scene the way they wanted it to look, then drew it. They also did creative dramatics, acting out the story, and some children wrote story variants during writer's workshop.

Creating Art Journals

I have recently started trying out a new activity to meld art and writing: journals made from old calendars, magazines, or catalogs. Each child chooses or brings in an old calendar, magazine, advertising brochure, or catalog. Children may paste in pages, add images or writing, or cut pieces out, creating something uniquely theirs without worrying over neatness and precision. As Matthew expressed it, "It's cool to get to make your own special book journal this way."

These creations may be used during random moments, art or writing centers, rainy days, and other times. Glue and scissors are needed. It is helpful to have colored pencils, marking pens, and other supplies. I also give children enlarged photocopies of our class picture to use in their writings and drawings.

Children may keep these art journals private or read or share them with others, as they wish.

Making Time and Space for Social Reading

Children need many different kinds of reading experiences. It is much easier for them to attempt to focus and read silently during sustained silent reading if other times are provided for them to read with a chosen friend or friends and to talk about books and reading. I try to make time for social reading available at least three times a week, as well as in literacy centers. Sometimes children need this time directly after silent reading—they are just bursting to talk about books.

One of the things children like best about social reading is that they may read with whomever they wish, or alone if they prefer. They select their reading materials and also choose *where* they will read.

Some days we brainstorm together about places we like to read. Francisco makes a cut-paper tree made of books. He adds a cut-out letter "r" and draws himself on top of it with some books. He explains that it is "a book house for reading in, 'r' is for 'read.'" Brenda writes about places where she likes to read:

> I like to read in my school.
> I like to read in my house.
> I like to read on my sofa.
> I like to read in my bed.
> I like to read in my book.

When children have a choice of where to read in the classroom, some read on the rug. Others sit on top of desks, at desks, or under desks. More private children read in the art alcove or a book corner. I look up to see Stephen intently reading his poetry book's table of contents by himself. Karen is reading to our largest stuffed animal, "the biggest bear," as she cuddles into him. Haneen lies down with Janet on the rug and they read and talk as they hold the books up overhead. A small group of boys, Oscar, Irving, Hugo, and Christian, riotously enjoy a story together, talking about it, laughing, reading some parts, and discussing illustrations.

Figure 5–1. Francisco's book house—a tree made of books!

Children are all over the room, reading and talking, with books as their focus. They really are intense about this experience. They are developing relationships with friends as readers—"making reading friends."

Working with Book Buddies

The children have another kind of social book experience once a week with their third-grade book buddies. Buddies are paired—each third grader works with a specific first grader each week. The buddies read to the children, talk to them about books, and encourage their emerging literacy as the year goes on. Children have a close relationship with their buddies. We do an occasional art lesson together, an end-of-the-year picnic, and sometimes a field trip. They share their personal writing in pairs and as a large group.

For more about some unusual and very involved cross-curricular book buddy activities and personal relationships, see the book *Surprising Destinations: Young Children on Track Toward Lifelong Learning* by Mary Kenner Glover and Beth Giacalone.

6

Leaping into Literacy Through Pictures and Photographs

I can go anywhere in my mind. The pictures I think can help me to go there.

—Ricky

Making Literacy Happen

First graders *want* to learn to read and my job is to help them *realize* this goal—to believe it and achieve it. To do this I need to keep a constant spotlight on the idea of learning to read by giving children time to talk about reading, think about it, and even draw pictures of themselves reading. This focus helps children to "see" themselves reading, and ultimately they do read.

Drawings, murals, poetry charts, and illustrated booklets are all ways of helping children to literacy. One day we wrote a class poem together and then made a mural to cement our ideas and visualizations. Our poem was about reading places. I wrote some of it and the children added bits and pieces and rhyming words. We agreed on this final form:

Reading Everywhere
I can read a book sitting with my bear,
I can read a book in a car, in a chair.
I can read a book with my best friend,
We can read a book all the way to the end.
I can read a book in my bed at night,
I can read a book on an airplane flight.
I can read a book when I'm here or there.
I can read good books everywhere!

We talk about this piece of writing and I print it on a large piece of nonfading mural paper. The children create illustrations to go with their new work of literature. Other ideas surface and are added to the poem and to the group of illustrations surrounding the words. This becomes a focal point in our classroom for several days. The intent of this activity is not to create a stunning piece of literature, but to become aware of all the places we can read. We play with these images and words and the ideas they evoke, and we create them visually. Having these personal ideas in front of us may spur children on to doing something they haven't done before: read in bed at night, read at the beach, read in a car or in a tree. I call these "visual motivators."

Using Visual Motivators

Our "places to read" mural is both a celebration of reading and a visual motivator. It is in front of us, spurring us on to think of and try out more and better places to enjoy reading. Another visual motivator is our "favorite books" panel: a six-foot red non-fading paper hanging illustrated with children's drawings of themselves and their favorite books.

We make many kinds of visual motivators together, from panels and murals to illustrated poetry charts, learning games, and class books. Often we use photographs of the children as ingredients in the visual motivators.

I believe that being able to "see"—visualize—yourself doing something makes it more possible to actually *do* that thing or achieve it in real-life situations. These visualizations can *predict* the experiences. With this in mind I start creating photo-art visual motivators early in the school year. The first one we make is a photo mural with the words "We Love to Read" painted (or printed on the computer) across the top. The mural has a photo of each child or small groups of children reading, alone or with friends. The children choose the book they'll be pictured with. The mural also has large-type dictated comments from children expressing their feelings about books and reading. Torn-paper figures of children with books can also be added. Using visual motivators, we project ideal situations and desired outcomes—and then they happen!

Enacting Poems and Rhymes

Early in the school year we make photo poetry charts. There are several parts to this process. These charts are made from poems, nursery rhymes, or book excerpts illustrated with children's art and the children's photographs. We make these with poems or rhymes we know well, so we learn and enact the poems first.

Nursery rhymes and songs are a good place to start. We say them, chant them, mime them, and sing them when possible. We let the words roll out of our mouths as we put action to them. Children choose favorites. They work in small groups. Each group portrays a particular rhyme with movement, dance, action, song, and creative dramatics. We make an "audience circle" and these group portrayals of

Figure 6–1. Reading mural: a visual motivator

rhymes are performed for the class. Props are sometimes created and used: puppets, a paper log or fence, a jump rope and an apple, and so forth.

Today, "five green and speckled frogs" sit on a student-made "speckled log" and pretend to be eating "some most delicious bugs" as they sing, chant, and munch. One by one they leave the log, and the group becomes smaller, until the frogs are all gone. They resurface to much applause.

For our next act, Maria recites indignantly the traditional rhyme "As I was standing in the street, as quiet as could be, a great big ugly man came up and tied his horse to me." Before she finishes speaking Jeremy comes along pulling another student (the horse) behind him with a jump rope. He ties the "horse" to Maria, gives her an apple, and falls over the rope as he pats the horse on the head. This is followed by several other acts, all depicting much loved, much appreciated rhymes and poems.

The next step, another day, is to "freeze the action." Each group creates a tableau of their chosen rhyme, poem, or song. Every child in the group gets into the best possible position to show the meaning of the rhyme. Everybody can be seen, and the tableau is a good composition. Children "freeze." *Now* I take a photograph. We have enjoyed creative dramatics and mime with the rhymes. Now when we have the photograph developed we can make an illustrated chart.

Making Poetry Charts

Manila chart paper (twenty-four by thirty-six inches is a good size) are colored poster board (twenty-two by twenty-eight inches) are both good backgrounds for photo poetry charts. I print the poem by hand right on the background paper, or type it in large print on the computer. With the poem or rhyme placed in the middle of the background paper, I put children's enlarged photographs near the text. I may cut around photos or leave them as is. Now I have children add the art. Sometimes at the beginning of the year I do the art.

To make a *Humpty Dumpty* photo chart (see Figure 6–2), a child posed and I photographed him with a digital camera. I made a large print of the photo on the computer and cut out the figure of the child. José Manuel decided he wanted to be sitting on the wall next to Humpty Dumpty. I attached his photo and glued on the large-type poem, and we made a few illustrations with oil pastels. Student

Figure 6–2. *Humpty Dumpty* photo poetry chart

art may be used instead of the teacher's. The best way to add student art to this type of chart is to use cut-paper student art or drawings made with oil pastels or marking pens. These are cut out and attached.

I try to stress with the children that when we are creating art, such as a poetry chart or mural, it is best to put down all the parts, move things around, and get a composition we like before we glue. When we make a chart or mural more permanent, we lift each piece, put glue or tape rolls under it, then press it back in place without moving it. In this way the composition is created *one* time, then made permanent just the way we like it.

The Process and the Product

When we made this *Humpty Dumpty* poetry chart it was early in the school year, and I did more of the art than I do later on. This is because I really wanted to have a *product*, a visual motivator I could use in the classroom. I wanted to create a chart that would have *intense* interest for the children because they knew the rhyme intimately and had enacted it, and also because their own photos were part of the illustration.

The children were more involved with the process of deciding how to enact the poem, and in the actual enactment. They were involved with literature interpretation. This is just one way to handle the making of photo poetry charts. Later on in the school year students are more involved with visual arts and their own creative expression because *they* are doing the art on a chart. In any case, I want the main focus for these chart-making sessions to be on the literature—the poetry and the rhyme—rather than the art activity itself.

At the time of the *Humpty Dumpty* chart we made five charts at once, with a different group of children featured in each poem or nursery rhyme. In this way each child in class had a place in a tableau, and all charts went on display. We refer to these charts often, saying the words as we track them with a pointer, admiring the charts and discussing our photographic illustrations. The charts are self-esteem builders, art gallery pieces, and predictors of reading achievement: They are great tools to motivate the children to read.

Going Beyond Poetry Charts

There are several other projects that relate to the poetry charts and use the photos already taken and poetry already learned. One project is our photo alphabet. The children enjoy placing cut-out photos near letters on a classroom alphabet strip to make a personalized alphabet. A variation of this photo alphabet is to make one or two alphabet letters for each child to hold, then take photos of each group of two to four children. Alphabet letter photos are placed in order above the chalkboard.

The poetry calendar is a logical extension of our enjoyment of poetry in the classroom. It is our classroom gift to our families for the winter holidays and the new year. Each month of the year is illustrated with a poem and a child's drawing.

Years ago when I first began making poetry calendars with my first graders I placed the September calendar page on each child's desk on the first day of school. I tried to teach the poem and prod the children to illustrate it for a present for their families. Of course this approach didn't work. I realized quite soon that I was the only person in the classroom who cared whether or not we illustrated the September poetry page on the first day of first grade. There was no benefit to the children in following through on my instructions, should that by some miracle have happened. After thinking about it I realized I was going against everything I believed about literacy by asking children to respond to a piece of literature that meant nothing to them.

I write about this incident with chagrin and some embarrassment to remind others (and mostly myself!) about the importance of keeping our educational goals in mind when we create literature extensions and response activities.

Now when I prepare the calendars I choose poetry and rhymes ahead of time based on poetry I want to teach early in the school year. I print and copy the calendars and keep them ready, stacked by month. About the beginning of November I share the calendar idea, and show the children a calendar page with a poem I know they love. They are *wild* to illustrate it, chant it, personalize the page, and get at it with crayons and marking pens. Eleven more pages will be done the same way, a page at a time, over about a month and a half of the first semester. These are much loved and agonized over. We keep them in individual file folders, one per child. As a class we look at and discuss individual children's art styles and chosen ways of illustration. We marvel at the many ways of seeing and interpreting a poem. And we celebrate everybody's artistic expression!

The completed calendars are put in order by the children and rechecked by me. Calendars get covered with green or blue nine-by-twelve-inch construction paper front and back. They are three-hole punched at the top. Red yarn is threaded through the left and right holes and tied in front with a bow. The center hole is for hanging the calendar. A copy of the child's school photo for the year is placed in the center of the cover. Children add festive details with cut paper or marking pens. The children take these calendars home to their families as gifts for the new year. The calendars are beautiful, but aside from the wonderful illustrations, the real gift children are taking home is the gift of sharing their reading and reciting of the poetry inside.

A focus for the end of the school year is the class photo poetry book. For this activity, the children each *choose* a poem, nursery rhyme, or book excerpt that is "really important" to them, one that they know and love. This is a culmination of our poetry study throughout the school year.

The leaves are feathers in the wind
I dance and swirl and make no sound.
The leaves fall gently through the sky
The leaves and I float to the ground.
—Pat Barrett Dragan
Starring Maggie Minero

Figure 6–3. Page from a photo poetry book

We brainstorm as a group to decide which poems to choose. I do not create the list. The children must bring out of themselves the poems they have learned that matter to them and then pick their own special one to illustrate. Usually there are a few children who want the same poem. Over the course of a few days these decisions can be worked out. Children may share a poem by illustrating it together, or divide it by each choosing a stanza. Children check the poetry books in the classroom libraries and also negotiate with each other to decide on other possible poems. After a week or so all the children have chosen their own special poems.

Mime the Rhyme!

Now, as with the poetry charts, each child decides how to mime the poem of choice. I photograph each child individually (together if they share a poem). Sometimes props are needed: a chair, if the poem requires sitting; the floor for flying or swimming; and so forth. I use color film, but I reproduce the class books in black and white. When the film is developed I cut out the photos of the children and give them out with rolls of tape on the back. The children place photos on the pages with the typewritten poetry, then draw the rest of the illustrations with thin black marking pens. I photocopy and spiral-bind these to make individual copies of our class photo poetry books.

A less expensive variation is to enlarge the class picture for the year on a copying machine and give the correct cut-out head photo to each child. Children draw the missing parts of themselves when they illustrate the poems.

Another related project is to have the children draw the cover of a book they love. They then make two or three paper props. For example, Matthew may draw the cover of *Where the Wild Things Are*. I photograph the book cover—either the one he has drawn or the actual cover of the book. I photograph Matthew wearing a paper crown and holding a paper scepter. When the film is developed the children create collage scenes, using the giant book photos and small photos of themselves. In this variation they are literally making themselves part of the book.

Another way to create this integrated picture-book-and-figure effect is to photograph each child miming the book character. Develop and cut out the photos, then attach them to paper. Children add details with pens or cut paper.

An important ingredient of the class photo poetry book is the table of contents. Each poetry page must be numbered and the poems listed in the table of contents. Many "table of contents" games can be played when the children receive their books.

On the day children receive their photo poetry books we read and enjoy them together. It is a real day of celebration. The children, after all, are book illustrators and also readers!

Figure 6–4. Matthew and Danny "get into" books they love

We choose poems for group reading by looking in the table of contents and picking by title, by illustrator, or by theme. We make up riddles about the poems: "Which poems have animals in them? Which poem is about the sun? Let's read the poem starring Samuel." The children are then free to read anywhere in the classroom, alone or with other children of their choice. Everyone is reading and celebrating, enjoying the words and the pictures and being together to share the experience. It is always one of my favorite days all year.

7

Making Sense of Text Through Creative Responses and Literacy Centers

There is a Magic Box I have and in that box there is a book. But it is not an ordinary book. Every time you read it a different story is in it.

—Maggie

Opening the pages of a book can lead to a magical experience: making meaning from little marks on a printed page. And in a sense, all readers find a different story in the pages of a book, depending upon the personal meaning and context they bring to the story. When readers talk about and compare their story interpretations as well as "visual pictures" of a story, they can "see" an incredible variety of quite personal literature responses. One of the most important things we do as teachers is to help children find meaning and have intellectual, emotional, and personal responses to literature. When we help children see possibilities, brainstorm ideas, then provide tools and time for creative expression, we help children mull over a story and play in its pages mentally to bring it to full meaning.

Connecting art to literature can be a lifesaver for some children. The arts can be translators that help children see the bigger picture, the gestalt. Art helps children unlock text. It provides another way of "seeing" and making meaning clear. As expressed by Marsha Oviatt, a reading specialist and school psychologist in Pacifica, California, "The House of Literacy has many doors, and one way in is art."

"Hanging Onto" Story

When Jane Yolen's book *Dragon's Blood* came out I read late into the night, even though it was a school night. I was so enamored of the small dragon in this first book of the Pit Dragon Trilogy that I couldn't stop thinking about it. I traveled in and out of the pages of the book for quite some time that evening in my mind. The next morning as I was getting ready for school I found myself scrambling through my jewelry box to find a small dragon pin to wear. I did some dragon drawings and three pages of writing before breakfast. During the day I had a real need to talk about the story with a friend at school. I hadn't let go of the book emotionally or intellectually and, without realizing it, I wanted to continue a relationship with it.

Retelling, writing, and art all play a part in this feeling of not wanting to let go of a special story. We need to give children a variety of tools to use to continue a relationship with a book they love: storytelling and retelling techniques, some art and bookmaking ideas, and varied writing instruction.

This is not to say that everyone who reads a book will make the same connections and will want to write about, talk about, or draw the main character or other parts of the story. That would take away the joy of discovery and creation. However, if we have the tools and some experiences in responding to literature in a variety of ways, we are more apt to be able to play and connect with the written word in ways that suit our own modalities, our learning intelligences.

Not doing an extension or book-based response should be a choice as well. Children who so choose could go on with reading books of their choice or write or reread for their own purposes. As we are all aware, reading responses need to be personally relevant to the learner.

Responding to Story in Literacy Centers

Literacy centers give children important opportunities to work on literacy skills and respond to literature in a variety of ways. I teach small-group guided reading during this hour-and-ten-minute time period. The first ten to fifteen minutes, those children not working directly with me read books from their "center-time book bags." These plastic freezer bags have children's names on them and contain some books of their own choice and some books they have previously read. The bags also contain four-page folded booklets of stories illustrated by children in the class. These are retellings of stories read in small-group guided reading. Each child has a personal bag.

The next part of the center time period lasts thirty to forty minutes. The children go to one assigned center. When they finish there they have five-plus free-choice centers from which to choose.

Assigned Centers

For the last ten minutes of center time each day, children assemble on the rug to share major work, problems, and successes. They bring their binders, folders, and art portfolios. Any center problems are ironed out here as well. I am working to photograph children modeling activities that can be done at each center. These will be put on small signs at the centers to help children "see" different ways to use their time. Other new ideas will be photographed as they evolve.

In general I find centers more successful, especially at the beginning of the year, if I limit the supplies and materials so that it is easier for children to stay focused. It is also easier to have fewer choices of materials when children are learning to take care of things and to put them away.

Center Assignments

Children are assigned to centers in groups of four or five. Names of children in each group are written on three-by-five cards. Center-group assignments are changed several times a year so children have opportunities to work with different classmates. Each center has a card with its name and appropriate illustration or photograph.

Center-group cards with the children's names are placed in a pocket chart on the top row. Cards for required centers are placed in the row underneath, right under the names of groups assigned to them. Free-choice center cards are placed in the bottom row. To change cards daily I move the top-right group card to the front (beginning at the left) and move other group cards down a space to the right.

My goals for the five main centers are that they focus on well-loved books chosen by the children and that they be somewhat generic. By generic I mean that any piece of literature of the child's choice could be "plugged in" to the center format. A final goal for me is that the centers take a minimum of planning and set-up time, and that they provide intense, real experiences for the children. The five main centers are the art center, the writing or bookmaking center, the poetry center, the word-collecting center, and the book talk and buddy reading center.

Art Center Children can use colored pencils, crayons, oil pastels, marking pens, and torn or cut paper to image their favorite book, setting, character, or story scene. I put a few supplies out at a time and vary them.

Ideas for this center vary to suit our curriculum and the specific interests of the children. Periodically other art materials are available at this center. I leave the children with suggestions and supplies for art lessons that have previously been taught. Once children know how to do an art activity they may do it (or try it again) at this center, hopefully using the time to respond to a favorite book. Different materials are available as they suit our needs: nonhardening plasticine clay, watercolors, oil pastels, and so forth.

Currently the children want to "be like Eric Carle" (their idea!). Many are trying out painted-paper collages after listening to *The Very Hungry Caterpillar*, *The Very Quiet Cricket*, and *The Very Busy Spider*. We previously painted our own decorative paper and did this type of collage as a whole-class art lesson. I saved a lot of the painted paper scraps for center use.

Sometimes the art center becomes what Kay Goines calls a "pen table." The children use butcher paper and marking pens to draw and write, collaboratively illustrating a large piece of paper. Often these papers are used to illustrate book excerpt or poetry charts. Sometimes they cover boxes of class supplies.

Children may spend some art center time in the library or at the book wagon choosing a book they wish to use as a focus. Their overnight books may also be used. When the art center alcove is available, children work there. Two times a week our speech therapist works there with a small group of children. During this time children work in another part of the classroom on a long plastic roll-up mat that can be placed on the floor.

The art center can also be used for a class book response, done daily by a group of children. For example, one group of children each day might work on a cut- or torn-paper mural. On Friday the entire class assembles the mural. Children may work together on creating illustrations for a class mobile or other joint project. The project is put together after everyone has had a turn.

Recently, after listening to the picture book *Frederick* by Leo Lionni, the children created large "Frederick" vignettes each day. Every group had an eighteen-by-twenty-four-inch background paper for scenes from the book. By the end of the week we had five mini-murals on a specific book theme. The following week, in these same small groups, we did interactive writing for each picture.

Writing or Bookmaking Center Children write stories of choice or responses to literature books, or write letters to book characters or authors, children in the class, or classroom animals on a theme of choice or a book-related theme. The center has different kinds of paper, stationery, old greeting cards, envelopes, and different kinds of writing materials: watercolor pencils, marking pens, and crayons. I try to reserve some materials, such as gel pens, black paper, glitter crayons, and rubber stamps, for children to use when illustrating their "published" books. Sometimes other kinds of paper will be available at this center, such as a paper with three boxes or parts for the children to write and draw in about the beginning, middle, and end of a special book.

Occasionally I make specific writing papers or books, one for each child, such as ready-to-go accordian-fold or zig-zag-fold books, stapled list books, pop-up books, folded four- or eight-page booklets, and stapled books of eight blank pages. Children keep all work from this center in writing folders.

Another option at this center: two children a day can write at the computers.

I find that some specific direction is needed at this center, particularly at the beginning of the school year. For example, when the children were so involved with our Eric Carle author study, they loved the idea of doing a book "Eric Carle style." They enthusiastically suggested several titles, including "The Very Piggy Pig," "The Very Hungry Shark," and "The Very Quiet Teacher." I added four-page booklets to the center, as well as plain paper, a stapler, and staples. Children were free to pursue their own writing ideas or use suggestions provided.

Another idea for the writing center is to unite it with a science center so children may have time for observation, writing and drawing, and perusing books on a specific subject. At this time of the school year children are using the writing/science center to observe caterpillars, chrysalids, and butterflies and write about and draw them. Several children are making their own butterfly books.

Poetry Center Children read and illustrate a different poem or book excerpt each week and put it in a poetry binder. Students also read poems on a poetry chart rack. They then rebuild the poem line-by-line in a pocket chart, using tagboard strips. There is a more challenging set of cut tagboard strips to use to rebuild the poem word-by-word. A good variation is to match cut words to sentence strips. I also include pointers at this center. I always stress the joy of rereading the poem.

The poetry center also contains large laminated envelopes of poetry. Each envelope has a poem printed on the front. The poem is reprinted in a different configuration on the back. There are illustrations to key children in to which poem they are reading. Inside the envelopes are both tagboard strips with lines of poetry and individual cut-out letters. These are for rebuilding the poem, using the envelope for reference. This envelope poetry activity is a smaller version of the poetry chart experience.

The poetry cube described in Chapter 4 may also be used at the poetry center. Children roll the cube and recite the poem that lands face-up. They may use several smaller cubes at a time or one large one. Poetry cubes (also called book excerpt cubes) are changed often.

Word-Collecting Center Children use a preprinted grid of four, six, or nine boxes for writing their words. The paper is three-hole punched. Children use dictionaries and favorite books to collect words they like. They print a word in a grid or box using a thin marking pen or colored pencil. Then the word is illustrated. Incomplete pages are kept at the center in a plastic bag. When a page is finished it is kept in the child's word-collecting binder. If binders are not available, folders will work, but they are harder to keep organized. I try to get used binder and folder donations from local businesses as well as from our school business partners.

Another word activity is to match words on three-by-five cards to labels around the room. The children can also collect words on a folded paper with cut flaps that lift up. Children may write a beginning sound or word on the front lift-up flap and make an illustration in the space underneath. A variation is to make booklets with one cut lift-up flap for each letter of a child's name. The children copy one letter from their names on each flap. They then write a word and draw a picture underneath. Another variation is to cut and paste words or pictures from magazines. Magazines, scissors, paper, and glue sticks are available at this center. Rubber alphabet stamps could be used for spelling words children like, such as words from favorite stories or the names of classmates, or high-frequency words on our word wall.

A more mobile variation of the word-collecting center is the reading scavenger hunt. I provide clipboards with pencils tied to them with lengths of yarn. Each clipboard contains a paper that lists words to be found or such puzzles as find words that begin with "w," have a long "a" vowel, or are scary (at Halloween). When children are finished they put their papers in their word-collection binders or folders.

Book Talk and Buddy Reading Center This center has some double or multiple copies of books children have already heard read aloud. Children have the option of reading to each other and talking about the stories or just talking about books and stories. They may do so in pairs or small groups. They may do this anywhere in the room as long as they do not bother children in other centers. Another activity children may do at this center is match tagboard strips with book titles on them to the books on the overnight book display shelves. They may also match book titles to category charts, as described in Chapter 4. Big books and pointers are also available for reading.

At the beginning of the year, children flounder at this center. They may seem totally confident and anxious to talk about books during DEAR time (sustained silent reading). However, it is quite another matter when talk is the focus of the center and "book talk" is what you want them to do.

I find it helpful to talk about this frequently before center time and direct children back to what we are working on in our literacy mini-lessons or guided reading groups. For example, I am working now on teaching children how to find meaning in books by relating them to their own lives. Relating books this way helps children practice this skill and have fun with it. We call this "making connections."

My first graders are beginning to be able to focus on this reading comprehension skill in small groups during centers. Recently I overheard several children talking about *Pierre* by Maurice Sendak, and relating their own stories about times when *they* had said "I don't care!" I was really pleased with the snatches of conversation I heard. Sometimes it pays to eavesdrop!

Recently, during parent conference week, a shortened day situation, I read several books to the children as they ate lunch. At the end of the read-aloud time Esmeralda said indignantly, "You forgot to ask us about our connections, and I have a really, really good one!" Set straight about this I immediately found time for "connection sharing."

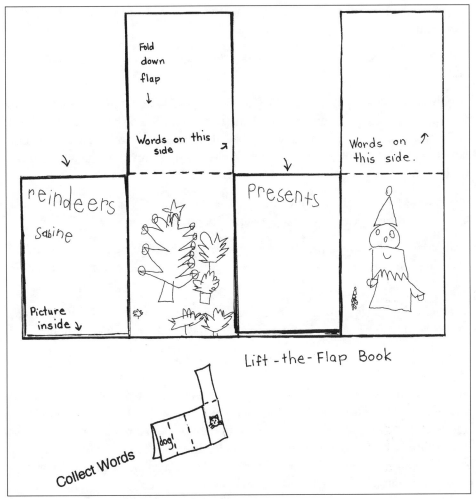

Figure 7–1. A lift-the-flap book

I have read more about finding personal relationships to text in *Mosaic of Thought: Teaching Comprehension in a Reader's Workshop* by Ellin Oliver Keene and Susan Zimmermann. I found it extremely helpful for showing children how to make meaning from text.

Free-Choice Centers

When children finish at their main centers they may go to a free-choice center. These are important centers as well. Sometimes I switch center-group assignment cards and these free-choice centers become the required first centers each day. My classroom has these free-choice centers:

Listening Center New literature books and tapes are available each week. Music "sing-alouds" are good for this center too.

Block Building Center Children build with wooden blocks and stuffed animals. I have taped poems, alphabet letters, and children's names on the sides and ends of some of the blocks. The basket of stuffed animals, a small briefcase of toy cars, or a tub of plastic dinosaurs can be used with the blocks if children wish. I vary the materials that are available.

Library Center Books are organized in tubs and also in large book displays. Big books are also available on two easels, with a variety of pointers nearby.

Book Wagon Center This is a mobile version of the library center. Children may *always* go to these centers to peruse and pick new books for their center-time book bags or to use at other centers.

Game and Toy Center This center offers a potpourri of different items children enjoy using according to their own interests, such as Legos, puzzles, magnetic letters, and board games.

Creative Dramatics Center In this center there are a variety of thematic materials and props for portraying a seasonal event, such as Halloween, a place to work, such as a doctor's office or grocery store, or a specific literature book. I keep these supplies in large envelopes and vary them throughout the year. I try to provide some books and literacy ideas for this type of center. For example, the children are currently enamored of the book *Sheep Out to Eat* by Nancy Shaw. The large envelope for this book contains restaurant menus, an apron, a towel, a notebook, and a pencil for a waiter to carry, paper plates, a few plastic food items, and copies of the book. Children love to reenact the book, especially the part where the waiter tosses the sheep out of the restaurant. The sheep are refused service for making a mess and not eating the food they mistakenly ordered because they could not read the menus. (Naturally I have a hidden agenda in using this piece of literature!)

This creative dramatics center lends itself to props made by children, such as varieties of menus, order forms, and advertising posters for specific foods, as well as coupons and play money. For many other ideas for this type of center see Gwen Owocki's book *Literacy Through Play*.

8

Retelling Stories

First I make it in my head, And then in my heart, And then in the paper.
—Gabriela

Retelling with Triaramas

I have just shown children the basic steps to make a "triarama," a folded triangle diorama. We brainstorm many ideas for using this simple form to showcase our own special books of choice. Children now know ways to create the basic form or variations of it, and have ideas for adding details of character or setting their own way. They are talking, experimenting, and going back and forth between book and art to create their own visualizations. Of course there are no right answers—just the thrill of making a personalized version of a story come to life.

At some point during the making of the triaramas some children will retell stories, using the triangle modules to scaffold their storytelling endeavor. Others may choose to write about the story or read related books from a nearby book tub. I want children to come up with their own ideas and have time to explore them.

Time is a key element: time for the relevance of a book to incubate within us as we live vicariously through its pages. Children also need time for working out not just their visions for the triaramas, but for figuring out technically how to create scenes and show off their ideas within the three-dimensional form.

This project may require two, three, or even more sessions until children are satisfied that things are finished. Pieces may be stored within the triangle forms for future use until the projects are complete. Sometimes I suggest that some children go back to their special books for more details to add. Children can talk and brainstorm together to see if their ideas and renderings are clear and if there are vital elements missing. As usual with an art experience, there will be children who finish early and those who need more time.

Recently I taught an English language unit about a forest and forest animals to a group of twenty children who were just beginning to learn English. Over a

period of several days they made triaramas in small groups as a culminating activity, talking as they worked, then practiced talking about the animals and the
forest environments in their triangles. The children worked together to retell the
forest story, using the triaramas to help them remember details, sequence, and
other story information. Each group decided on their own triangle formation, and
as it turned out, each configuration was different. And each group of children suc-
ceeded in the creative process, the language experience, and the interpersonal
group experience. The art project scaffolded—supported—children's language
learning.

I will never forget the first time I taught this triarama project. It was around
the time of the summer Olympic Games several years ago and we had read in a
children's magazine about some of the specific events going on. Many of my first
graders were extremely involved in creating sports scenes, and I was standing back
marveling at all the critical thinking skills they were using. Tony asked me about
attaching a basketball hoop off the edge of the triarama so that his character could
really "shoot high." I never did understand *exactly* what he wanted, but I valiantly
suggested several techniques to him, mostly paper strip supports, and even a craft
stick with a hoop on top of it glued to the back of the triarama. I tried very hard
to brainstorm ideas with and for Tony, and was feeling creative, nurturing, even
helpful—for about two minutes. "Oh, that's okay," he said, and walked away to
develop an incredible triarama, far beyond the ideas of his first-grade teacher.

Making Triaramas

To create a triarama we use nine-inch- or twelve-inch-square construction paper.
We fold it on the diagonal two times to make a folded "X." Then we cut from
one corner to the center, and fold to overlap.

I show children, and we brainstorm, a few ways to attach figures and objects
to the triangle three-dimensionally, with flaps that bend and are glued, with paper
strips, and even by cutting pop-up boxes into the triangle form. A pop-up box
may be cut into any inside fold (any fold that will end up inside the triangle form).
See Figures 8–1 and 8–2 for ideas.

Now children are well equipped with a variety of techniques. Using a lot of
critical thinking skills and rereading relevant parts of books they have chosen,
they create a favorite scene, a character, a mood, and so on. Children may cut or
tear the scene from construction paper, use magazine cut-outs, and use collage or
any other techniques they have learned or innovated. Art may be attached to the
triangle inside and out. Photographs or copies of photos may also be used. Written
descriptions or stories may also be attached.

Using Triaramas in a Family Literacy Program

I used this project as part of a Family Literacy Night program at my school. Parents and children became very involved in it. Magazines were a popular way into the project for adults who may have felt uncomfortable drawing. I felt that many families would continue working on their triaramas at home, and would later add relevant items such as photos or copies of photos. I also enjoyed the family talk going on between parents and children as they worked on the projects together. These very personal verbal interactions between parents and children may have been the most important part of the evening.

Finishing Early

Children, and in fact all of us, can benefit from the opportunity to do things again when they finally understand how to do them. Creating a second or even a third project with a similar scene or with variations is a good learning experience for children who have finished ahead of the rest. Children gain increasing confidence with each creative project they work on, especially if they have set the goals themselves.

Another valuable experience for early finishers is to *draw* their completed triaramas. I have learned many valuable tips about art from my art mentor, Dick Sperisen, who is art coordinator emeritus at the San Mateo County Office of Education in California. According to Dick, when children have been intimately, kinesthetically involved with a three-dimensional project, they gain much from really looking at it—*seeing it*—then reproducing it in a two-dimensional medium such as a drawing. Children can add paper scraps, crayon, or marking pen to drawings, or do a series of two-dimensional cut- or torn-paper reproductions of their three-dimensional work. Children can also be encouraged to write about their visual creations. The writing can be copied into a booklet (four-page, eight-page, or other style) to put on display next to the completed triangle modules.

Configuring Triaramas

A triarama project can be done effectively and quickly using single modules. However, once in a while you may wish to go all out for the multiple module effect. The intriguing thing about these triangle forms is that they can be placed many ways to reflect varied types of ideas. For example, if you place four of them together back to back, you get a completed form. A set of four lends itself to ideas such as using one module each to represent the book title and the beginning, middle, and end of a story. Another idea is to have one module each for the character, setting, plot, and resolution. Children could create four triaramas, or could

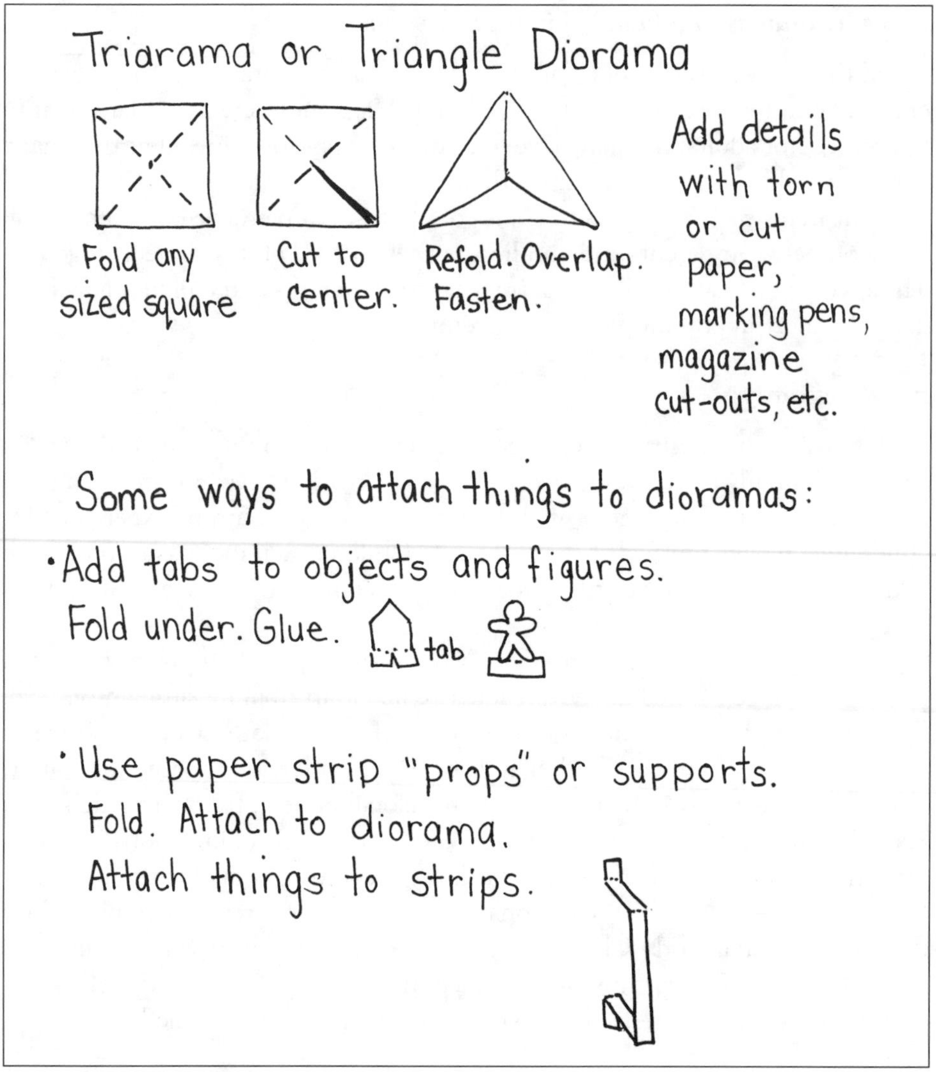

Triarama or Triangle Diorama

Fold any sized square

Cut to center.

Refold. Overlap. Fasten.

Add details with torn or cut paper, marking pens, magazine cut-outs, etc.

Some ways to attach things to dioramas:

• Add tabs to objects and figures. Fold under. Glue. tab

• Use paper strip "props" or supports. Fold. Attach to diorama. Attach things to strips.

Figure 8–1. Making and configuring triaramas

work in small groups to represent parts of a book. The modules may be glued together or fastened temporarily with paper clips or a temporary sticking material.

If single triangle modules are created, one way to display them in front of a window or on a table is to place one face-out in front of a window and the next one face-in, alternating the alignment. In this way there is something interesting to look at on both sides of a table, or both inside and outside of a room.

If children are working with such books as *Tops and Bottoms* by Janet Stevens, a good configuration is to place one triarama on top, right-side up, with another

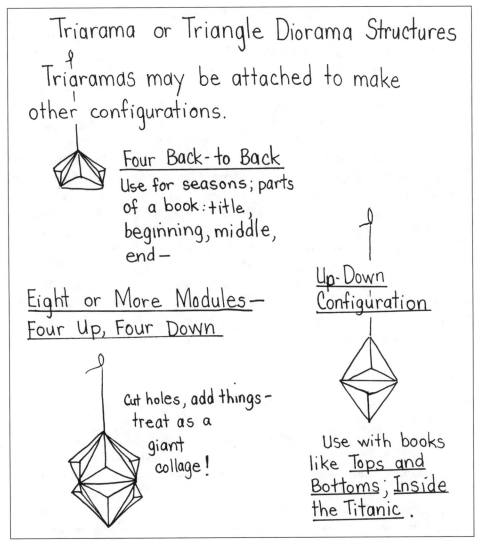

Triarama or Triangle Diorama Structures

Triaramas may be attached to make other configurations.

Four Back-to Back
Use for seasons; parts of a book: title, beginning, middle, end —

Eight or More Modules —
Four Up, Four Down

Cut holes, add things — treat as a giant collage!

Up-Down
Configuration

Use with books like *Tops and Bottoms*; *Inside the Titanic*.

Figure 8–1. Continued

attached to it upside down. The growing of different vegetable crops can be shown in this way, especially the root crops that figure so importantly in this trickster tale. The tops of vegetables can be shown in the top triarama, and parts of vegetables that grow underground can be shown in the bottom module. This up-and-down format also lends itself well to a book like *Mike Mulligan and His Steam Shovel*. Use the top triarama for ground level and the bottom triarama for the cellar where Mike and Mary Anne are trapped. Part of the cellar "floor" could be cut out. The up-and-down format could also be used with *Inside the Titanic* by

Ken Marschall, *Polar the Titanic Bear* by Daisy Spedden, *Swimmy* by Leo Lionni, or any other book with an underwater scene. The upper triarama shows the water surface and sky, while the lower, upside-down, triarama shows what is going on under the surface of the water.

These top-and-bottom scenes may be hung on strings or pieces of yarn, or pinned to a bulletin board (with pins in the center points of the triangles to create a three-dimensional display). To make a more complicated version, do a grouping of four right-side-up modules and attach another four upside down.

My first graders and I created a wonderfully wild scene for Eric Carle's book *The Very Hungry Caterpillar* using multiple triaramas. We made eight triangle modules. We made pop-up boxes in some of them by cutting boxes into the folded edges, then poking them through to the other side. We also cut some holes in the triangle forms, then glued eight forms together, four right-side up, four upside down. By now the structure was a little unwieldy, very bulky, and had to hang by a piece of yarn so that we could work on it. The resulting project was incredible! The very hungry caterpillar wandered through holes and pop-up box openings and among all kinds of paper food. We even glued on tiny labels so that the caterpillar would know what it had eaten. We had different caterpillars in different scenes, in a range of sizes to represent our growing insect. Finally, we had a *giant* caterpillar, then—a large and very beautiful butterfly!

Multi-Module Variation This eight-module structure could be used as a whole-class project for any theme or unit of study. For example, it could be developed to show the many levels of Hogwarts, the wizard school attended by Harry Potter and friends in J. K. Rowling's books. If used with a resource book such as *Children Just Like Me: Celebrations* by Anabel Kindersley, each module could show a how a child lives in another country, or modules could show a variety of celebrations around the world. Individual triarama modules could be used for group projects about a specific novel. Each person in the group could develop a module about a chapter or different literary element. Another variation would be to use the project with alphabet books such as *The Accidental Zucchini: An Unexpected Alphabet* by Max Grover or *Chicka Chicka Boom Boom* by Bill Martin Jr. and John Archambault. Use these books to create an "alphabet habitat" showcasing all the letters of the alphabet.

Whatever ways an art or writing project is used in the classroom the *key* is showing children *how* to make something and then letting them make the connections and decide on the direction and development of the project. These artistic triarama renditions of a story are fun in themselves, but many times they help make the meaning of the book or details clear, and enable children to get more out of the reading experience.

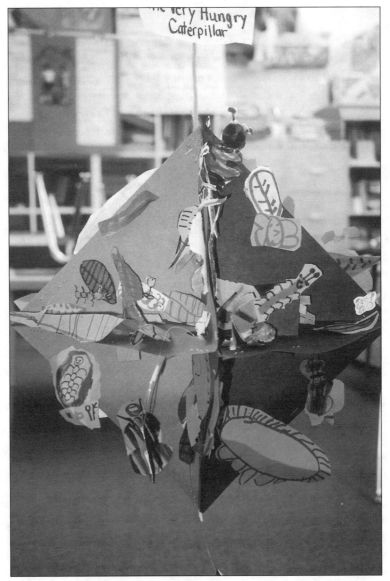

Figure 8–2. Eight triaramas put together

Retelling Stories in Many Ways

One of the powerful things that happens when children share books is that they begin talking about the books and connecting what they read to their own experiences, their own lives. In the process of this shared time they are *retelling* stories. They are practicing *visualizing* stories. This helps them to remember details and story sequence. Retelling is a way of revisiting the story, enjoying it again in a new way. Reflecting and retelling activities strengthen reading comprehension and memory. They help children understand how stories are structured and organized, how story language works, and how to use language creatively.

Before children retell a story they need to hear it many times and live inside it in their minds. They need scaffolding—group experiences in how to retell, what to practice, and what to include. *Revisit, Reflect, Retell: Strategies for Improving Reading Comprehension* by Linda Hoyt has a multitude of strategies for helping children learn this important skill. There are many types of retellings, including the following.

Artful Retellings

I like to use art as a way to retell and visualize a story or book. I choose the media, such as marking-pen drawings, torn paper or tempera paint, and children use both words and pictures in their retellings of portions of the story. We place these visual images (and later, typed words as well) in order as a group. These are glued to a large piece of colored nonfading mural paper or manila chart paper. We enjoy revisiting the story as a group as we admire our art, our wonderful words, and our creative expression.

Story-Board Retellings

One method I have used to help children retell a much loved story is to draw three boxes on a strip of paper. Children draw, then talk about, the beginning, middle, and end of a story.

The Envelope Theater

A follow-up to the story-board activity is the "envelope theater." Teachers or parents can cut a two-by-two-inch square opening in the mailing address side of an envelope. Cut off the envelope ends and glue the envelope flap closed. Children can illustrate a story sequence on adding machine tape, then run the story from left to right through their "theaters." The ends of longer pieces of adding machine tape may be glued together to make a continuous story loop. Children love retelling their stories this way, with friends in attendance.

Figure 8–3. A retelling of *Little Lumpty*

Personal Retellings

I like to help children with retelling and sequence by relating things to their own lives. I give each child three four-by-six-inch cards or six-by-nine-inch pieces of construction paper. The children think about and draw the three most important times in their lives. They place the papers or cards in order from left to right according to what happened first, second, and third. The pictures are glued together in order to make a very personal time line. A variation is to have children organize these drawings top to bottom and hang them on a length of yarn or ribbon.

Creative Dramatics

Creative dramatics is one way of retelling a story. Children can live and play through a story they know, remembering sequence, details, characters, and setting. This is described in Chapter 4 in the discussion of the presentations of *Pierre*.

Booklet Retellings

Another method I have used to help children retell a well-loved story is to draw eight large boxes on the whiteboard and help the group block out the story. One box is for the title. We then fill in each box with a sentence or two from the beginning, middle, and end of the story. Then we fill in details about character, setting, story problem, or most important happening. We use the information in the eight boxes to retell the story together.

Later in the day or that evening I reformat the story boxes into an eight-page booklet (see Appendix 3). I create a booklet, then open it, and copy in the words and phrases from the rough-draft boxes made in class. I start with the title in the second box from the bottom and go counterclockwise. (Four-page booklets may be used if eight-page booklets seem too complicated. Save a page each for title, beginning, middle, and end.)

When the booklet is complete I make photocopies and fold a booklet for each child. Children then read, retell, and illustrate the story. The booklet becomes a keepsake or artifact of the whole experience. Children may keep their booklet collections in plastic bags, folders, or small "bookshelves" made from empty gelatin boxes. In these boxes, the booklets are reminiscent of Maurice Sendak's *Nutshell Library* of four tiny books in a slipcase.

Puppet Theaters and Craft-Stick Puppets

Easy puppet theaters may be made by the children to use with their own retellings of favorite books. This week as I reread *The Three Billy Goats Gruff* I created a puppet theater and puppets for characters and scenery. I folded a twelve-by-eighteen-inch piece of construction paper in half widthwise and cut a "theater opening" that looks like curtains in the front half. I "talked the book" to the children so they could see my thinking about which characters and parts of settings I decided to use for puppets. Ultimately I drew, cut, and attached several figures to craft sticks to make puppets: three billy goats gruff, the troll, the bridge, a hill with no grass, and a hill with green grass. I placed the uncut half of the twelve-by-eighteen-inch paper on a desk so the cut-out theater curtains hung down over the desk opening. To perform the story I sat under the student desk so that the

Figure 8–4. An under-the-desk puppet show

paper theater curtains framed the puppet show. I retold *The Three Billy Goats Gruff*, holding up characters and background props as needed.

My performance drew rave reviews and my first graders were wild to make their own theater and puppets for their favorite books. I sometimes give children a pattern for the theater opening, but this time I had precut them, which took only seconds because I cut five at a time. (See Appendix 5 for theater pattern.)

As children busily went to work thinking and creating Matthew said, "I don't want any sticks. I don't need them." He couldn't quite express what he was going to do instead but he obviously had a plan. "I want to do it *my* way," he said. "Aha!" I thought, my own words coming back to haunt me. But I really was delighted. I very much want the children to approach art as well as writing in a truly creative and personal way.

When the children performed their plays from under a desk at the end of the period they sat behind their theater curtain openings and moved their puppets as they retold their tales. The rest of us sat on the rug to watch and listen. When it was Matthew's turn, he put his theater on top of the desk face down and stood by the desk. At the midpoint of his retelling he stood the theater upright dramatically, and the crayoned troll under a bridge could be seen on the back flap of the theater structure. Matthew continued his retelling to much applause. This variation worked for Matthew, and the children and I were impressed that he had thought of another way to make the project work.

I gave each child a large plastic bag to hold the theater and puppets. The next day our weekly newsletter, the *Braggin' Dragan*, explained the project to parents and suggested that they request a puppet show. Children took home their bags, which also contained folded papers for another theater and characters, as well as several craft sticks.

9
Writing Our Way

*When I write something I get a picture and colors in my brain and I think
of the words and the writing comes out of my pencil.*

—Sabine

Conquering Fears and Getting Excited About Learning

Reading and writing are linked in children's minds as something they are going
to learn right away in first grade. With this in mind I have my first graders jump
right into writing the first day of school. Since children find it very hard to write
when they are worried that they need to know how to spell and how to form letters, the initial hurdle is getting something down on paper. Fortunately, the blank
page is easily conquered with drawings. Children can be quite prolific in drawing, a feat I tell them scares many adults. This familiarity and comfort level with
drawing helps ease them into writing. When children are *really* reluctant to get
anything down on that vast blank expanse, I sometimes tell them that their words
are already down there in the paper. All they have to do is make marks "their
way" and the words will be there. Later on I say, "Write the sounds you hear."

I want the children to be excited about writing both at home and at school.
Each day a child is chosen to take home the class lizard, a large key chain with a
plastic lizard that I purchased inexpensively at the student store. The lizard lives
in a paper bag with a felt-tip pen, inside a binder. Children clamor to take the
lizard home and write and draw its adventures. The next day the lizard's escapades
are read to the class.

I used to send home a teddy bear with a journal and backpack full of clothes.
However, all the children wanted to sleep with the teddy bear and colds spread
rapidly. The class lizard prefers to sleep alone in its paper bag. I now have a variety
of plastic figures and binders that go home.

Teaching Children to Do It Their Own Way: Writer's Workshop

As teachers in a variety of school districts in many geographical locations, we may
be required to teach a particular curriculum, such as a specific reading, phonics,

Matthew_Matthew_
Matthew's story about the
"Class Lizard".

the Lizard is going
to Hawaii. He is looking
for shells.

Figure 9–1. Matthew's "class lizard" journal page

writing, and spelling series. My own school district has a required curriculum. I do my own program, as detailed in this book, in addition to what is required, integrating everything as much as possible

I rely heavily on the work of Lucy Calkins, Donald Graves, and other notable educators in the reading, writing, and language arts field in planning and implementing my own writer's workshop. Since so many expert books, workshops, and materials are available (see the Reading Resources list), I won't elaborate much here.

My personal twist when I teach writer's workshop is to say to children beginning to write, "Write it *your* way!" I have said and demonstrated this idea many ways in the classroom each year, but this sentence seems to free children up to be themselves in the evolving writing process. I hear them repeating it to themselves and each other throughout the school year, almost like a mantra or "magic feather" granting them permission.

I have shown my first graders a variety of ways that children write "their way" when beginning to write, from assorted scribbles and pictures to symbols, strings of letters, beginning and ending sounds, bits of words, whole words mixed with other things, and actual sentences. I show them a piece of my early writing, from age two—not quite a scribble even. We talk about how we were not all born the same day and how we don't all talk, walk, or grow at the same time either. And we talk about how we certainly *don't* have to be able to write and spell at the same time *now*.

In case these little demonstrations do not seem to take, I have a few of the stuffed animals in the class "write it their way." I hold the animal and write for it to demonstrate rabbit's way, bear's way, spider's way, and so on. The children tell me what the animal is trying to write, and I do a variety of writing, as just described. This helps to get the idea across. I mention to my class that the spider does a little more reading and writing than the other creatures in the classroom at night, so its way of spelling is a little closer to the regular spelling the children will learn later.

Using Interactive Writing

We do interactive writing, working together to write meaningful text on a large piece of chart paper. As children take turns writing we figure things out and fix some words and punctuation with opaque white "magic fixing tape," taping over one error at a time and correcting it. The point of this is to be free to *begin* to write without having to be perfect at it right away.

Banana Breath, my stuffed gorilla, often comes to visit at this point to demonstrate "interactive gorilla writing." I write for Banana Breath as the children tell me what to say. Then we fix the spelling together with the "magic fixing tape"

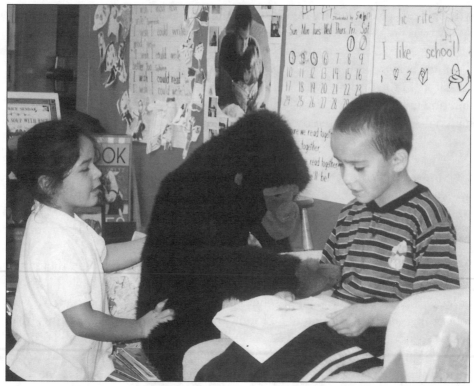

Figure 9–2. Reading to Banana Breath

or small computer labels. Children then go to their seats to draw and write something that's really important to them, and Banana Breath goes around and tries to "read" from their papers. He seems particularly interested in the work that has both drawings and tries at writing. At the beginning of writers' workshop children are much less intimidated about sharing their work with a stuffed gorilla than with me. After all, they already shared his struggles to write "his way." In this manner we work and play our way to literacy.

Banana Breath leads the way for many first graders to begin writing. One early writing activity is to write to one of the myriad of stuffed animals in the classroom. Children love doing this kind of writing in small booklets. I make a variety of different sizes so they have choices. They enjoy "reading" their stories back to the animals later. If the reading isn't accurate, nobody tells.

Often at the beginning of writer's workshop the children cannot read their hard-won writing. We struggle, looking at it together. Then I say things like, "Just think, Tyler! You are the *only* person in the *whole world* who knows what this says! It is like a secret code! You are the only person who can read it." Sometimes this loosens things up. Tyler can make up whatever he likes: Who would know what the writing originally said?

Organizing Children's Writing

Some of the early literacy mini-lessons I teach deal with the idea that the stories we read aloud have beginnings, middles, and ends. When we begin writing the children are given a set of four stapled unlined papers. On the first page they "write," draw, or list four or more things they know or care enough to write about. These are their "expert topics." The next three pages are for writing and drawing their stories. This idea, emphasizing a beginning, middle, and end, can evolve into a story that will be edited and published.

Each child is then given a writer's notebook of 50 spiral bound pages. These are stored in a hanging folder in a plastic crate. Later in the year, after we start using the word wall for high-frequency words, children will also have writing folders for word lists and works in progress. I make each folder by cutting a standard two-pocket folder in half. I use one half, pocket side up, per writing folder. To keep children focused, only writing that's in progress is kept in the pocket. Other writing is either published or kept in the hanging folders. Some children find the packet cumbersome and use the writer's notebook for ongoing work. Children need both the writer's notebook and the folder.

I three-hole punch the completed work-in-progress writing folder and use brads to hold these materials (in order):

> One clear plastic transparency. This serves as a cover and allows easy access to word-wall words.
> List of word-wall words. This includes words that have been introduced, which children highlight using highlighter pens or yellow crayons.
> Two papers for a personalized word list. The list consists of each child's personal frequently used words.
> Half of a pocket folder, pocket side up.

Children who are particularly interested in learning new words often like to find words they need on the word-wall list. Many other word-wall ideas may be found in *Phonics They Use: Words for Reading and Writing* by Patricia M. Cunningham.

Getting into the Story: Children's Writing Influences

As the beginning of the school year progresses, I see many connections between the children's writing and finished products and both the Overnight Book Program and the poetry we are learning. Often children write further adventures of characters they love, or write sequels or parallel books. Sometimes they choose characters from two or more books or poems and write about adventures they have together. Some children put themselves into these adventures with the characters—they image themselves right into the stories.

This year at the beginning of the fall semester José Manuel chose the nursery rhyme *Humpty Dumpty* to "be part of." He mimed the rhyme and I photographed him for the *Humpty Dumpty* poetry chart. This experience turned out to be a powerful motivator for his first tries at writing. He was so consumed with writing about his imaginary (and very real!) conversations with Humpty Dumpty that it carried him over that difficult time when children worry about what and how to write.

On the first day, José Manuel showed me a very involved drawing of Humpty Dumpty falling off the wall. He shared strings of letters he had written and explained worriedly, "I told him, now don't wiggle and you won't fall!" José Manuel had drawn a ladder against the wall so that Humpty Dumpty would have a safe way down.

The following day the writing was even more involved, and Humpty's ally confided that he had told Humpty not to move. "I keep telling him, 'DON'T MOVE!' "

José Manuel wrote further about the experience and even placed a stop sign on top of the wall to ward off the inevitable. José Manuel was clearly inside the imaginary world of the nursery rhyme. By the third and fourth days he had invented a reason for Humpty Dumpty's accident: He had bitten José, who was now happy to see him fall. In the final stories the egg had been put back together again "with fruit drivers" (I think this means *screwdrivers*), and was starring in a Humpty Dumpty show! Humpty Dumpty cookies were sold to the people who watched the show.

I was astonished at the detail in these daily sagas, most of the story told through strings of letters. There was considerable interest on the part of the class in these pieces of writing and the incredibly involved drawings. Several other children began writing and drawing their own *Humpty Dumpty* variations. In Lupita's version, Humpty Dumpty falls from her bunk bed but does not break. He stays on to play with her. Henry gives Humpty a magic cape and the ability to fly. And Luis gives him "a ladder to the sky" and friends from other nursery rhymes to play with.

First graders are sometimes so involved with favorite books and stories that the line between story and classroom reality is blurred. This was the case with Oscar and the main character of his favorite book, *Avocado Baby*, written and illustrated by John Burningham. Avocado Baby is a very strong baby in a weak

Figure 9–3. José Manuel's *Humpty Dumpty* story

family. He chases a burglar away and even protects his older siblings from bullies by throwing the bullies into a pond.

One day I was struggling to move a heavy bookcase in the classroom. Oscar looked over at me and remarked, "Avocado Baby could do that." Oscar organized and played Avocado Baby games at recess. He wrote and shared several *Avocado Baby* variants and sequels. He even sent some to John Burningham along with a note asking for more Avocado Baby stories. I believe that Oscar structured his whole world around *Avocado Baby*. The book gave form and meaning to his life. As stories can do for all of us, it helped him create *who* he is, to make sense of the world and his place in it.

Helping Children Through the Writing Process

As with literature and art, I feel that my role in the writing process is to give children the tools and strategies they need, then let them go to work on things close to their own hearts. As I conference with children I try to help by questioning and listening to them express what they are trying to write. I try to have a very accepting, nonthreatening presence so that I don't get in the way. I want children to feel the power of their own discoveries and listen to their own inner voices. That way what they create will be uniquely theirs.

Finishing Their Own Books

Another hump to get over in the writing process is getting ready to publish. It helps to have a wonderful assortment of art supplies ready for publishing and illustrating, the dessert at the end of the writing struggle.

When the children work individually with me to edit their work we focus on one or two important items at the child's personal writing level, such as correct use of periods and capital letters, and correct spelling of word-wall words.

I help each child create a short author/illustrator biography on the final page of the book. The child's class picture is added here. If a classmate has written a critique of the work we include it on this page.

When the book is ready for publishing I type it on the computer and make two copies, one for our classroom library and one for the child to take home. Both copies get spiral bound or stapled with a construction paper or laminated construction paper cover.

Children illustrate their published books by choosing from such materials as metallic colored pencils, watercolor pencils, gel pens, glitter crayons, metallic crayons, rubber stamps, stickers, crayons, and marking pens. Some prefer other techniques we have learned, such as torn-paper collage. They *love* being illustrators.

Celebrating Publication

We celebrate the publication of each new book by having the child sit in the author/illustrator's chair and read to the children in our class as well as to our visiting book buddies. A few times each year parents are invited to an author/ illustrator celebration. One copy of the completed book is added with ceremony to our classroom library. Many children will choose it to take home "for overnight." The author's name, book title, and photo are all added to our prominently displayed class chart. We read the chart together with pleasure. The chart is titled "The Author Came Today!"

Reading Resources

Resources for Teachers

Reference Books

Avery, C. 1993. *And with a Light Touch: Learning About Reading, Writing, and Teaching with First Graders*. Portsmouth, NH: Heinemann.

Calkins, L. M. 1994. *The Art of Teaching Writing*. Portsmouth, NH: Heinemann.

Cunningham, P. 1999. *Phonics They Use: Words for Reading and Writing*. New York: Addison-Wesley.

Gardner, H. 1993. *Frames of Mind: The Theory of Multiple Intelligences*. New York: Basic Books.

———. 2000. *Intelligence Reframed: Multiple Intelligences for the 21st Century*. New York: Basic Books.

Giblin, J. C. 1993. *The Riddle of the Rosetta Stone: Key to Ancient Egypt*. New York: HarperTrophy.

Glover, M. K., and B. Giacalone. 2000. *Surprising Destinations: Young Children on Track Toward Life-long Learning*. Portsmouth, NH: Heinemann.

Graves, D. 1987. *Writing: Teachers and Children at Work*. Portsmouth, NH: Heinemann.

Hock, B. V. 1999. *The Labyrinth of Story: Narrative as Creative Construction*. Ph.D. diss., University of San Francisco.

Hoyt, L. 1999. *Revisit, Reflect, Retell: Strategies for Improving Reading Comprehension*. Portsmouth, NH: Heinemann.

Keene, E., and S. Zimmermann. 1997. *Mosaic of Thought: Teaching Comprehension in a Reader's Workshop*. Portsmouth, NH: Heinemann.

Owocki, G. 1999. *Literacy Through Play*. Portsmouth, NH: Heinemann.

Peterson, R., and M. Eeds. 1990. *Grand Conversations: Literature Groups in Action*. New York: Scholastic.

Visual and Performing Arts Framework for California Public Schools, Kindergarten Through Grade Twelve. 1996 Sacramento, CA.

Books About Choosing Books

Hearne, B., with D. Stevenson. 2000. *Choosing Books for Children: A Commonsense Guide.* 3d ed. Champaign-Urbana, IL: University of Illinois Press.

Hopkins, L. B. 1998. *Pass the Poetry Please!* New York: HarperCollins.

Lewis, V. V., and W. M. Mayes. 1998. *Valerie and Walter's Best Books for Children: A Lively Opinionated Guide.* New York: Avon Books.

Trelease, J. 1994. *The Read-Aloud Handbook.* 4th ed. New York: Penguin Books.

Videos

The Bring Me a Book™ Foundation in Palo Alto, California, has produced several videos to inspire teachers and parents to read quality literature to children of all ages. These include

The Art of Using Poetry in the Classroom. 1999. Presented by Ellen Lerner. Consultant: Kay Goines.

The Book Envelope: An Overnight Connection. 2001. Created by Kay Goines. Presented by Paula Walling, Lisa Meckel, Pat Barrett Dragan, Kathy Bauer, and Celeste Dueber.

Bring Me A Book™ Library: A Model Library in the Workplace for Employees and Their Children. 1998. Presented by Kay Goines.

Family Literacy Night. 2001. Presented by Rosellen Mastoris. Consultant: Kay Goines.

Magazines

Book Links: Connecting Books, Libraries, and Classrooms. Published 6 times a year by Booklist Publications, P.O. Box 615, Mt. Morris, IL 61054-7564. American Library Association, 50 E. Huron Street, Chicago, IL 60611.

The Horn Book Guide to Children's and Young Adult Books. Published twice a year by The Horn Book, Inc., 56 Roland Street, Suite 200, Boston, MA 02129.

The Horn Book Magazine. Published six times a year by The Horn Book, Inc.

The Horn Book Guide, Interactive CD-ROM. 1998. Portsmouth, NH: Heinemann. The Horn Book, Inc.

School Library Journal. Published 12 times a year by Cahners Business Information, 245 W. 17th Street, New York, NY 10011.

Books for Children

Books Mentioned in the Text

Ada, A. F. 1997. *The Lizard in the Sun/La lagartija y el sol.* New York: Bantam.

Burningham, J. 1982. *Avocado Baby*. New York: HarperCollins.

———. 1997. *The Shopping Basket*. Cambridge, MA: Candlewick.

Burton, V. L. 1999. *Mike Mulligan and His Steam Shovel*. Boston: Houghton Mifflin.

Cannon, J. 1993. *Stellaluna*. New York: Harcourt Brace.

Carle, E. 1969. *The Very Hungry Caterpillar*. New York: Scholastic.

Cohen, M. 1989. *When Will I Read?* New York: Aladdin.

Duvoisin, R. 2000. *Petunia*. New York: Knopf.

Gag, W. 1956. *Millions of Cats*. New York: Paperstar.

Galdone, P. 1981. *The Three Billy Goats Gruff*. Boston: Houghton Mifflin.

———. 1984. *The Three Little Pigs*. Boston: Houghton Mifflin.

Henkes, K. 2000. *Wemberley Worried*. New York: Greenwillow.

Hoff, S. 1999. *Danny and the Dinosaur*. New York: Harper Festival.

Imai, M. 1996. *Little Lumpty*. New York: Candlewick.

Kantrowitz, M. 1976. *Willy Bear*. New York: Parents' Magazine Press.

Kraus, R. 1988. *Leo the Late Bloomer*. New York: HarperCollins.

Lionni, L. 1987. *Frederick*. New York: Knopf.

——— . 1992. *Swimmy*. New York: Knopf.

Lowell, S. 1992. *The Three Little Javelinas*. New York: Northland.

Marschall, K. 1997. *Inside the Titanic*. Boston: Little, Brown.

Marshall, J. 1974. *George and Martha*. Boston: Houghton Mifflin.

Naylor, P. 1994. *King of the Playground*. New York: Aladdin.

Raffi. 1992. *Five Little Ducks*. (Raffi Songs to Read.) New York: Crown.

Rathman, P. 1995. *Office Buckle and Gloria*. New York: Scholastic.

Sendak, M. 1986. *Nutshell Library: Chicken Soup with Rice, Pierre, Alligators All Around, One Was Johnny*. (Boxed set.) New York: HarperCollins.

———. 1988. *Where the Wild Things Are*. New York: HarperCollins.

———. 1991. *Pierre: A Cautionary Tale in Five Chapters and a Prologue*. New York: HarperCollins.

Spedden, D., 1994. *Polar the Titanic Bear*. New York: Little Brown.

Stevens, J. 1995. *Tops and Bottoms*. New York: Harcourt Brace.

Waddell, M. 1994. *Can't You Sleep, Little Bear?* Cambridge, MA: Candlewick.

———. 1996. *Farmer Duck*. Cambridge, MA: Candlewick.

Wells, R. 1999. *Emily's First 100 Days of School*. New York: Hyperion.

———. 2000. *Timothy Goes to School*. New York: Viking.

Wolo. 1946. *Sir Archibald*. William Morrow and Company, Inc. Reprint 1992. Livingston, MT: Clark City Press.

Yolen, J. 1996. *Dragon's Blood*. Vol. 1 in the Pit Dragon Trilogy. New York: Harcourt Brace.

Zelinsky, P. 1990. *Wheels on the Bus: The Traditional Song*. Pop-up edition. Adapted and Illustrated by Paul O. Zelinsky. New York: Dutton.

Books by Category

Lullabies and Bedtime Books

Aliki. 1968. *Hush Little Baby.* New York: Simon & Schuster.

Brown, M. W. 1991. *Goodnight Moon.* New York: HarperCollins.

Burningham, J. 1999. *Husherbye.* London: Jonathan Cape/Random House.

Frazee, M. 1999. *Hush Little Baby—A Folk Song with Pictures.* New York: Browndeer Press.

Ho, M. 2000. *Hush! A Thai Lullaby.* New York: Orchard.

Long, S. 1997. *Hush Little Baby.* San Francisco: Chronicle Books.

Music Picture Books: Sing-Alouds and Chants

Aliki. 1974. *Go Tell Aunt Rhody.* New York: Macmillan.

Brett, J. 1997. *The Twelve Days of Christmas.* New York: Paperstar.

Carle, E. 1997. *Today Is Monday.* New York: Paperstar.

Guthrie, W., illustrated by K. Jakobsen. 1998. *This Land Is Your Land.* Boston: Little Brown.

Langstaff, J. 1974. *Oh, A-Hunting We Will Go.* New York: Atheneum.

Manson, C. 1993. *The Tree in the Wood: An Old Nursery Song.* New York: North-South.

Raffi. 1988. *Wheels on the Bus.* Raffi Songs to Read. New York: Crown.

———. 1997. *Baby Beluga.* Raffi Songs to Read. New York: Crown.

———. 1990. *Down by the Bay.* Raffi Songs to Read. New York: Crown.

Seeger, P. 1994. *Abiyoyo.* New York: Macmillan.

Nursery Rhymes

Cousins, L. 1989. *The Little Dog Laughed and Other Nursery Rhymes.* New York: Dutton.

Long, S. 1999. *Sylvia Long's Mother Goose.* San Francisco: Chronicle Books.

Marshall, J. 1996. *James Marshall's Mother Goose.* New York: Farrar, Straus and Giroux.

Opie, I., ed. 1996. *My Very First Mother Goose.* Cambridge, MA: Candlewick.

———. 1999. *Here Comes Mother Goose.* Cambridge, MA: Candlewick.

Tripp, W. 1973. *A Great Big Ugly Man Came Up and Tied His Horse to Me.* Boston: Little Brown.

Wildsmith, B. 1996. *Mother Goose.* New York: Oxford University Press.

Poetry

deRegniers, B., ed. 1988. *Sing a Song of Popcorn: Every Child's Book of Poems.* New York: Scholastic.

Hall, D., ed. 1999. *The Oxford Illustrated Book of American Children's Poems.* New York: Oxford University Press.

Hoberman, M. A., ed. 1994. *My Song Is Beautiful: Poems and Pictures in Many Voices.* Boston: Little Brown.

James, S., ed. and illus. 1999. *Days Like This—A Collection of Small Poems*. Cambridge, MA: Candlewick Press.

Kennedy, X. J., and D. M. Kennedy, ed. 1992. *Talking Like the Rain—A Read-to-Me Book of Poems*. New York: Little Brown.

Livingston, M. C. 1987. *Celebrations*. New York: Holiday House.

Lobel, A. 1988. *Whiskers and Rhymes*. New York: Morrow.

McCord, D. 1967. *Every Time I Climb a Tree*. New York: Little Brown.

Prelutsky, J., ed. 1983. *The Random House Book of Poetry for Children*. New York: Random House.

———. 1986. *Read Aloud Rhymes for the Very Young*. New York: Knopf.

———. 1999. *The 20th Century Children's Poetry Treasury*. New York: Random House.

Schields, C. D. 1998. *Month by Month a Year Goes Round*. New York: Dutton.

Worth, V. 1987. *All the Small Poems*. New York: Farrar, Straus and Giroux.

Alphabet Books

Anno. 1975. *Anno's Alphabet*. New York: Crowell.

Ehlert, L. 1989. *Eating the Alphabet: Fruits and Vegetables from A to Z*. San Diego: Harcourt Brace.

Grover, M. 1993. *The Accidental Zucchini: An Unexpected Alphabet*. New York: Harcourt Brace.

Lionni, L. 1990. *The Alphabet Tree*. New York: Knopf.

Lobel, A. 1981. *On Market Street*. New York: Greenwillow.

Martin, B., and J. Archambault. 2000. *Chicka Chicka Boom Boom*. New York: Aladdin.

McDonnell, F. 1997. *Flora McDonnell's ABC*. Cambridge, MA: Candlewick.

Sendak, M. 1992. *Alligators All Around*. New York: Scholastic.

Shannon, G. 1996. *Tomorrow's Alphabet*. New York: Greenwillow.

Counting Books

Anno. 1986. *Anno's Counting Book*. New York: HarperTrophy.

Bang, M. 1991. *Ten, Nine, Eight*. New York: Mulberry.

Demi. 1986. *Demi's Count the Animals 1-2-3*. New York: Grossett.

Morozumi, A. 1990. *One Gorilla*. New York: Farrar, Straus and Giroux.

Sendak, M. 1992. *One Was Johnny*. New York: Scholastic.

Tudor, T. 2000. *1 Is One*. New York: Simon & Schuster.

Walsh, E. S. 1995. *Mouse Count*. New York: Voyager.

Colors

Crews, D. 1978. *Freight Train*. New York: Scholastic.

Ehlert, L. 1989. *Color Zoo*. New York: Lippincott.

Lobel, A. 1968. *The Great Blueness and Other Predicaments*. New York: HarperCollins.

Walsh, E. S. 1995. *Mouse Paint*. New York: Voyager.

Predictable Books: Cumulative Patterns

Aardema, V. 1992. *Bringing the Rain to Kapiti Plain: A Nandi Tale*. New York: Dial.

Ahlberg, J., and A. Ahlberg. 1996. *Each Peach, Pear, Plum*. New York: Viking.

Carlstrom, N. W. 1996. *Jesse Bear, What Will You Wear?* New York: Macmillan.

Charlip, R. 1987. *Fortunately*. New York: Aladdin.

Dragonwagon, C. 1989. *This Is the Bread I Baked for Ned*. New York: Macmillan.

Emberley, B. 1967. *Drummer Hoff*. New York: Prentice-Hall.

Fox, M. 1986. *Hattie and the Fox*. New York: Bradbury Press.

Galdone, P. 1984. *Henny Penny*. Boston: Houghton Mifflin.

Kent, J. 1971. *The Fat Cat*. New York: Scholastic.

Martin, B. 1970. *Brown Bear, Brown Bear, What Do You See?* New York: Holt.

Neitzel, S. 1998. *The Jacket I Wear in the Snow*. New York: Greenwillow.

Numeroff, L. J. 1985. *If You Give a Mouse a Cookie*. New York: Harper & Row.

Pomerantz, C. 1974. *The Piggy in the Puddle*. New York: Macmillan.

Robart, R. 1987. *The Cake That Mack Ate*. Boston: Little Brown.

Rosen, M. 1992. *We're Going on a Bear Hunt*. New York: Scott Foresman.

Sendak, M. 1987. *Chicken Soup with Rice*. New York: Scholastic.

Sierra, J. 1998. *The House That Drac Built*. New York: Voyager.

Tabak, S. 1997. *There Was an Old Lady Who Swallowed a Fly*. New York: Viking.

Titherington, J. 1986. *Pumpkin, Pumpkin*. New York: Mulberry Books.

Tolstoy, L. 1968. *The Great Big Enormous Turnip*. New York: Franklin Watts.

Van Laan, N. 1987. *The Big Fat Worm*. New York: Knopf.

Viorst, J. 1996. *My Little Sister Ate One Hare*. New York: Crown.

Westcott, N. 1993. *I Know an Old Lady Who Swallowed a Fly*. New York: Harcourt Brace.

Wood, A. 1984. *The Napping House*. New York: Harcourt Brace.

Predictable Books: Participation Books with Rhythm, Rhyme, and Repetition

Alborough, J. 1992. *Where's My Teddy?* Cambridge, MA: Candlewick.

Asch, F. 1982. *Happy Birthday, Moon*. New York: Scholastic.

Brown, M. W. 1949. *The Important Book*. New York: Harper & Row.

———. 1994. *Four Fur Feet*. New York: Hyperion.

Burningham, J. 1970. *Mr. Gumpy's Outing*. New York: Holt.

———. 1978. *Would You Rather?* New York: Crowell.

deRegniers, B. 1955. *What Can You Do with a Shoe?* New York: Harper & Row.

Fleming, D. 1992. *In the Tall, Tall Grass*. New York: Holt.

Guarino, D. 1989. *Is Your Mama a Llama?* New York: Scholastic.

Hoberman, M. A. 1992. *A House Is a House for Me*. New York: Viking.

Joosse, B. 1991. *Mama, Do You Love Me?* New York: Scholastic.

Krauss, R. 1945. *The Carrot Seed*. New York: Scholastic.

Lionni, L. 1994. *Inch by Inch*. New York: Scholastic.

Mahy, M. 1987. *17 Kings and 42 Elephants*. New York: Dial.

Merriam, E. 1994. *Train Leaves the Station*. New York: Holt.

Shaw, C. 1947. *It Looked Like Spilt Milk*. New York: Harper & Row.

Shaw, N. 1989. *Sheep in a Jeep*. Boston: Houghton Mifflin.

———. 1992. *Sheep Out to Eat*. Boston: Houghton Mifflin.

Van Laan, N. 1990. *Possom Come a-Knockin'*. New York: Knopf.

Zolotow, C. 1958. *Do You Know What I'll Do?* New York: Harper & Row.

Books About Reading

Bradley, M. 1993. *More Than Anything Else*. New York: Orchard.

Bunting, E. 1990. *The Wednesday Surprise*. New York: Clarion.

McPhail, D. 1993. *Santa's Book of Names*. Boston: Little Brown.

Mora, P. 1997. *Tomas and the Library Lady*. New York: Knopf.

Stanley, D. 1999. *Raising Sweetness*. New York: Putnam.

Waber, B. 2000. *The Mouse That Snored*. New York: Walter Lorraine.

Wells, R. 1999. *Read to Your Bunny*. New York: Scholastic.

Books About Writing

Ada, A. F. 1994. *Dear Peter Rabbit*. New York: Atheneum.

———. 1998. *Yours Truly, Goldilocks*. New York: Atheneum.

Ahlberg, J., and A. Ahlberg. 1986. *The Jolly Postman, or Other People's Letters*. Boston: Little Brown.

Brown, M. 1996. *Arthur Writes a Story*. Boston: Little Brown.

Caseley, J. 1991. *Dear Annie*. New York: Greenwillow.

Cronin, D. 2000. *Click, Clack, Moo: Cows That Type*. New York: Simon and Schuster.

Heide, F. P. 1995. *The Day of Ahmed's Secret*. New York: Mulberry.

James, S. 1996. *Dear Mr. Blueberry*. New York: Aladdin.

Moss, M. 1955. *Amelia's Notebook*. Berkeley, CA: Tricycle.

Spinelli, E. 1996. *Somebody Loves You, Mr. Hatch*. New York: Aladdin.

Williams, V., and J. Williams. 1988. *Stringbean's Trip to the Shining Sea*. New York: Morrow.

Books About Drawing

dePaoli, T. 1997. *The Art Lesson*. New York: Putnam.

Fanelli, S. 1995. *My Map Book*. New York: HarperCollins.

Johnson, C. 1977. *Harold and the Purple Crayon*. Series. New York: HarperCollins.

McPhail, D. 2000. *Drawing Lessons from a Bear*. Boston: Little Brown.

Williams, V. 1986. *Cherries and Cherry Pits*. New York: Greenwillow.

Books About Books

Aliki. 1987. *How a Book Is Made*. New York: HarperCollins.

Stevens, J. 1995. *From Pictures to Words: A Book About Making a Book*. New York: Holiday House.

Books About School

Burningham, J. 1999. *John Patrick Norman McHennessy: The Boy Who Was Always Late*. New York: Dragonfly.

Calmenson, S. 1998. *The Teeny Tiny Teacher: A Teeny Tiny Ghost Story, Adapted a Teeny Tiny Bit*. New York: Scholastic.

Cohen, M. 1980. *First Grade Takes a Test*. New York: Greenwillow.

———. 1989. *Will I Have a Friend?* New York: Dell.

Henkes, K. 1996. *Chrysanthemum*. New York: Mulberry.

———. 1996. *Lilly's Purple Plastic Purse*. New York: Greenwillow.

Penn, A. 1993. *The Kissing Hand*. Washington, D.C.: CWLA Press.

Slate, J. 1996. *Miss Bindergarten Gets Ready for Kindergarten*. New York: Dutton.

———. 2000. *Miss Bindergarten Stays Home from Kindergarten*. New York: Dutton.

Books About Authors and Illustrators

Christelow, E. 1993. *What Do Illustrators Do?* New York: Clarion.

———. 1995. *What Do Authors Do?* New York: Clarion.

Cummings, P., ed. 1992. *Talking with Artists*. Vol. 1. New York: Bradbury Press.

———. 1995. *Talking with Artists*. Vol. 2. New York: Simon & Schuster.

———. 1999. *Talking with Artists*. Vol. 3. New York: Clarion.

dePaola, T. 1999. *26 Fairmont Ave*. New York: Putnam.

Lester, H. 1997. *Author: A True Story*. Boston: Houghton Mifflin.

Marcus, L. 1998. *A Caldecott Celebration*. New York: Walker.

McPhail, D. 1996. *In Flight with David McPhail: A Creative Autobiography*. Portsmouth, NH: Heinemann.

Books About Families

Cooke, T. 1994. *So Much*. Cambridge, MA: Candlewick.

Dorros, A. 1997. *Abuela*. New York: Puffin.

Hall, D. 1979. *The Ox-Cart Man*. New York: Viking.

Henkes, K. 1995. *Julius, the Baby of the World*. New York: HarperCollins.

Hest, A. 1995. *In the Rain with Baby Duck*. Cambridge, MA: Candlewick.

Hoban, R. 1995. *Bedtime for Frances*. New York: HarperCollins.

Kindersley, A., and B. Kindersley. 1997. *Children Just Like Me: Celebrations*. New York: Dorling Kindersley Publishing Inc.

Kraus, R. 2000. *Whose Mouse Are You?* New York: Simon & Schuster.

Lyon, G. E. 1993. *Come a Tide*. New York: Orchard.

McBratney, S. 1995. *Guess How Much I Love You?* Cambridge, MA: Candlewick.

Minarik, E. H. 1978. *Little Bear*. New York: HarperCollins.

Mitchell, M. K. 1998. *Uncle Jed's Barbershop*. New York: Aladdin.

Rosenberg, L. 1997. *Monster Mama*. New York: Putnam.

Rylant, C. 1993. *The Relatives Came*. New York: Aladdin.

Soto, G. 1993. *Too Many Tamales*. New York: Putnam.

Steig, W. 1989. *Sylvester and the Magic Pebble*. New York: Aladdin.

———. 1998. *Pete's a Pizza*. New York: HarperCollins.

Viorst, J. 1969. *I'll Fix Anthony*. New York: Aladdin/Macmillan.

Waddell, M. 2000. *Owl Babies*. Cambridge, MA: Candlewick.

Wells, R. 1973. *Noisy Nora*. New York: Dial.

———. 1992. *Hazel's Amazing Mother*. New York: Pied Piper.

Williams, V. 1982. *A Chair for My Mother*. New York: Mulberry.

Family Stories and Memoirs

Aliki. 1998. *Marianthe's Story: Painted Words/Spoken Memories*. New York: Greenwillow.

Garza, C. L. 1993. *Family Pictures/Cuadros de mi familia*. San Francisco: Children's Book Press.

———. 1996. *In My Family/En mi familia*. San Francisco: Children's Book Press.

Hearne, B. 1997. *Seven Brave Women*. New York: Greenwillow.

Ringgold, F. 1991. *Tar Beach*. New York: Crown.

Rylant, C. 1992. *When I Was Young in the Mountains*. New York: Dutton.

Books About Friendship

Allard, H., and J. Marshall. 1997. *Miss Nelson Is Missing*. Boston: Houghton Mifflin.

Blegvad, L. 2000. *First Friends*. New York: HarperCollins.

deRegniers, B. 1972. *May I Bring a Friend?* New York: Atheneum.

Heine, H. 1997. *Friends*. New York: Aladdin.

Henkes, K. 1997. *Chester's Way*. New York: Mulberry.

Hoberman, M. A. 1999. *And to Think That We Thought We'd Never Be Friends*. New York: Crown.

Lionni, L. 1993. *Little Blue and Little Yellow*. New York: Scholastic.

Lobel, A. 1970. *Frog and Toad Are Friends*. Series. New York: HarperCollins.

Steig, W. 1992. *Amos and Boris*. New York: Sunburst.

Varley, S. 1992. *Badger's Parting Gifts*. New York: HarperCollins.

Books About Special Characters

Bemelmans, L. 1939. *Madeline*. New York: Viking.

Bottner, B. 1992. *Bootsie Barker Bites*. New York: Putnam.

Burningham, J. 1994. *Courtney*. New York: Crown.

Cooney, B. 1982. *Miss Rumphius*. New York: Penguin Putnam.

dePaola, T. 1988. *Strega Nona*. New York: Aladdin.

Henkes, K. 1996. *Lilly's Purple Plastic Purse*. New York: Greenwillow.

Hoffman, M. 1991. *Amazing Grace*. New York: Dial.

Houston, G. 1992. *My Great-Aunt Arizona*. New York: HarperCollins.

Lawson, R. 1936. *The Story of Ferdinand*. New York: Viking.

Lester, H. 1990. *Tacky the Penguin*. Boston: Houghton Mifflin.

Lester, J. 1994. *John Henry*. New York: Dial.

Meddaugh, S. 1992. *Martha Speaks*. Boston: Houghton Mifflin.

Parish, P. 1963. *Amelia Bedelia*. New York: Harper Collins.

Potter, B. 1902. *The Tale of Peter Rabbit*. London: Warne.

Rey, H. A. 1941. *Curious George*. Boston: Houghton Mifflin.

Seuss, Dr. 1957. *The Cat in the Hat*. New York: Random House.

Steig, W. 1982. *Doctor DeSoto*. New York: Farrar, Straus and Giroux.

———. 1988. *Brave Irene*. New York: Farrar, Straus and Giroux.

Zion, G. 1956. *Harry, the Dirty Dog*. New York: Harper.

Books for Days When Everything Goes Wrong

Raffi. 1990. *Shake My Sillies Out*. Raffi Songs to Read. New York: Crown.

Seuss, Dr. 1957. *How the Grinch Stole Christmas*. New York: Random House.

Viorst, J. 1972. *Alexander and the Terrible, Horrible, No Good, Very Bad Day*. New York: Aladdin.

Wells, R. 1992. *Voyage to the Bunny Planet: First Tomato, Moss Pillows, Island Light*. Boxed set. New York: Dial.

Folklore and Fairy Tales

Aardema, V. 1980. *Why Mosquitos Buzz in People's Ears*. New York: Scholastic.

———. 1991. *Borreguita and the Coyote: A Tale from Ayutla, Mexico*. New York: Knopf.

Aylesworth, J. 1998. *The Gingerbread Man*. New York: Scholastic.

Brett, J. 1992. *Goldilocks and the Three Bears*. New York: Putnam.

Cohn, A., ed. 1993. *From Sea to Shining Sea: A Treasury of American Folklore and Folk Songs for All Ages*. New York: Scholastic.

dePaola, T. 1981. *Fin M'Coul, the Giant of Knockmany Hill*. New York: Holiday House.

Galdone, P. 1985. *The Little Red Hen*. Boston: Houghton Mifflin.

Hyman, T. S. 1983. *Little Red Riding Hood*. New York: Holiday House.

Kellogg, S. 1987. *Chicken Little*. New York: Morrow.

Kimmel, E. 1990. *Anansi and the Moss-Covered Rock*. New York: Holiday House.

Marshall, J. 1994. *Hansel and Gretel*. New York: Dial.

McDermott, G. 1988. *Anancy the Spider: A Tale from the Ashanti*. New York: Holt.

———. 1993. *Raven: A Trickster Tale from the Pacific Northwest*. New York: Harcourt Brace.

Polacco, P. 1988. *Rechenka's Eggs*. New York: Philomel.

Scieszka, J. 1989. *The True Story of the Three Little Pigs*. New York: Puffin.

Sierra, J. 1996. *Nursery Tales Around the World*. New York: Clarion.

Slobodkina, E. 1947. *Caps for Sale: A Tale of a Peddler, Some Monkeys, and Their Monkey Business*. New York: Scott.

Spirin, G. 1999. *Jack and the Beanstalk*. New York: Philomel.

Steptoe, J. 1985. *The Story of Jumping Mouse*. New York: Lothrop Lee and Shepard.

———. 1987. *Mufaro's Beautiful Daughters*. New York: Lothrop Lee and Shepard.

Tabak, S. 2000. *Joseph Had a Little Overcoat*. New York: Viking.

Tresselt, A. 1989. *The Mitten: An Old Ukranian Folk Tale*. New York: Mulberry.

Van Laan, N. 1998. *So Say the Little Monkeys*. New York: Atheneum.

Young, E. 1989. *Lon Po Po: A Red-Riding Hood Story from China*. New York: Philomel.

Zelinsky, P. 1986. *Rumpelstiltskin*. New York: Puffin.

———. 1994. *Swamp Angel*. New York: Dutton.

———. 1997. *Rapunzel*. New York: Dutton.

Chapter Books to Read Aloud

Atwater, R., and F. Atwater. 1938. *Mr. Popper's Penguins*. Boston: Little, Brown.

Bond, M. 1960. *A Bear Called Paddington*. Boston: Houghton Mifflin.

Cleary, B. 1996. *Ramona the Pest*. New York: Camelot.

Juster, N. 1993. *The Phantom Tollbooth*. New York: Random House.

King-Smith, D. 1993. *Babe, the Gallant Pig*. New York: Crown.

Norton, M. 1953. *The Borrowers*. New York: Harcourt Brace.

Rowling, J. K. 1998. *Harry Potter and the Sorcerer's Stone (Book 1)*. New York: Scholastic/ Arthur A. Levine.

———. 1999. *Harry Potter and the Chamber of Secrets (Book 2)*. New York: Scholastic/ Arthur A. Levine.

———. 1999. *Harry Potter and the Prisoner of Azkaban (Book 3)*. New York: Scholastic/ Arthur A. Levine.

———. 2000. *Harry Potter and the Goblet of Fire (Book 4)*. New York: Scholastic/Arthur A. Levine.

Seldon, G. 1960. *The Cricket in Times Square*. New York: Farrar, Straus and Giroux.

White, E. B. 1952. *Charlotte's Web*. New York: HarperCollins.

Other Classic Children's Literature

Anderson, H. C., and J. Pinkney, illus. 1999. *The Ugly Duckling*. New York: Morrow.

Brown, M. W. 1974. *The Runaway Bunny*. New York: HarperCollins.

———. 1995. *The Dead Bird*. New York: HarperTrophy.

Burdett, F. H. 1962. *The Secret Garden*. New York: Lippincott.

Flack, M. 1977. *The Story About Ping*. New York: Viking.

Gardiner, J. 1980. *Stone Fox*. New York: HarperCollins.

Graham, K. 1933. *The Wind in the Willows*. New York: Scribner.

Keats, E. J. 1981. *The Snowy Day.* New York: Puffin.

Kipling, R., and B. Moser, illus. 1996. *Just So Stories.* New York: Morrow.

MacLachlan, P. 1985. *Sarah, Plain and Tall.* New York: HarperCollins.

McCloskey, R. 1943. *Make Way for Ducklings.* New York: Viking.

Milne, A. A. 1992. *Pooh's Library: Winnie-the-Pooh, The House at Pooh Corner, When We Were Very Young, Now We Are Six.* Boxed set. New York: Puffin.

Moeri, L. 1975. *Star Mother's Youngest Child.* Boston: Houghton Mifflin.

Van Allsburg, C. 1985. *The Polar Express.* Boston: Houghton Mifflin.

Yashima, T. 1976. *Crow Boy.* New York: Viking.

Zolotow, C. 1985. *William's Doll.* New York: HarperTrophy.

———. 1990. *Mr. Rabbit and the Lovely Present.* New York: HarperCollins.

Appendix 1

School Book Clubs

School book clubs are an exciting and inexpensive way for children to buy books. The catalogs or magazines come out every three weeks or monthly. The teacher then sends them home, collects orders and money, and sends everything to the book club. Books are sent to the school and delivered to the teacher, who distributes them. The process can be time-consuming, but it gets children very excited about ordering and reading books. Teachers earn bonus points that can be used toward free books and other products.

It is a great moment when the book club package arrives. I always make a point of ordering a few things for the classroom, or to add to the overnight book collection. That way the box is for everyone in the room, and we *all* get mail!

The book clubs can also help teachers keep abreast of newly issued paperback books. The club magazines also have author and illustrator interviews and other helpful information for teachers.

These are the main school book clubs I use:

Scholastic Book Club
Phone: 800-SCHOLASTIC (800-724-6527)
Online: www.scholastic.com/bookclubs

Trumpet
Phone: 800-826-0110
Online: www.trumpetclub.com

Troll
Phone: 800-541-1097
Online: www.troll.com

Appendix 2

Classroom Materials

Book Displays

Calloway House has a large variety of fiberboard organizers, such as the large book displays I use in my classroom.

Calloway House, Inc.
451 Richardson Dr.
Lancaster, PA 17603-4098
Phone: 800-233-0290
Fax: 717-299-6754
Online: www.callowayhouse.com

Art Materials

Discount School Supply carries the liquid watercolors mentioned in Chapter 4. These watercolors are wonderfully vivid. They may be used alone or mixed with shaving cream.

Discount School Supply
P.O. Box 7636
Spreckels, CA 93962-7636
Phone: 800-627-2829
Fax: 800-879-3753
Online: www.earlychildhood.com

I use Fun-Tac reusable adhesive to hang artwork and put artwork together (affixing parts of a mural on background paper and so forth). Several companies have similar products, available at teacher supply stores and hardware stores.

DAP Incorporated
2400 Boston Street, Suite 200
Baltimore, MD
Phone: 800-543-3840 ×2804 or 888-327-8477
Online: www.DAP.com

Book Covers

Gaylord Bros. sells a wide variety of materials for covering and protecting books, including plastic covers and rolls of plastic in assorted sizes. Probably the easiest material for all-around classroom use is the 12-inch-by-100-yard roll of book jacket covers. It is helpful to share a roll and the cost with another teacher. Better yet is for the school to purchase a roll for all teachers to use.

Gaylord Bros.
P.O. Box 4901
Syracuse, NY 13221
Phone: 800-448-6160
Online: www.gaylord.com

Another material for covering books is clear adhesive plastic, also called laminating paper. This can be found in most large hardware stores and in school supply stores. There are many different brands, including Con-Tact.

Appendix 3

Making an Eight-Page Booklet

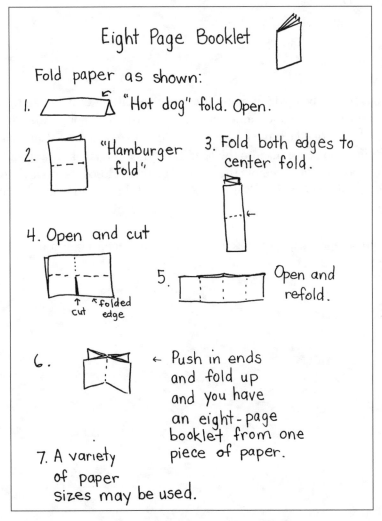

Eight Page Booklet

Fold paper as shown:

1. "Hot dog" fold. Open.

2. "Hamburger fold"

3. Fold both edges to center fold.

4. Open and cut

↑ cut ↗ folded edge

5. Open and refold.

6. ← Push in ends and fold up and you have an eight-page booklet from one piece of paper.

7. A variety of paper sizes may be used.

A variety of paper sizes may be used. I prefer copier paper because it is inexpensive, easy to fold, and can be photocopied when the booklet is completed. Twelve-by-eighteen-inch construction paper is good for larger projects.

Appendix 4

Making a Poetry Cube

Poetry cubes may be made in many sizes, using a variety of boxes and even milk cartons. I use two half-gallon milk cartons to make a small cube. After the cartons are washed and dried I cut the bottoms off to form two open-ended cubes. I squeeze and push until one cube fits into the opening of the other, making a six-sided cube.

To use boxes I simply empty them and tape them closed. Boxes are often more rectangular than cubic. This is not a problem: Children can make the cubes roll no matter what the shape.

To cover a completed cube, I wrap it in butcher paper in the same way I would wrap a gift. I tape the paper closed, then use wide tape to fasten it securely.

Appendix 5

Pattern for Puppet Theater Opening

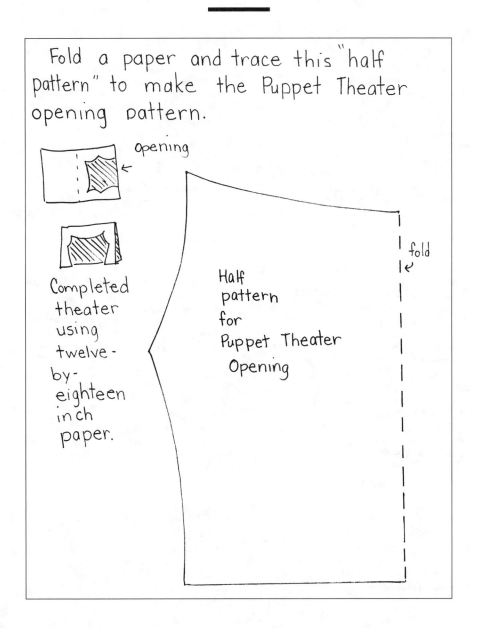

Fold a paper and trace this "half pattern" to make the Puppet Theater opening pattern.

opening

Completed theater using twelve-by-eighteen inch paper.

Half pattern for Puppet Theater Opening

fold

Index